# SAN FRANCISCO SECRETS

*Fascinating
Facts about the
City by the Bay*

John Snyder

CHRONICLE BOOKS
SAN FRANCISCO

Library of Congress Cataloging-in-Publication Data:
Snyder, John, 1951–
San Francisco secrets: fascinating facts about the city by the bay / John Snyder.
p. cm.
ISBN-13: 978-0-8118-2222-0    ISBN-10 0-8118-2222-2
1. San Francisco (Calif.) — Miscellanea.  I. Title.
F869.S345S69  1999                                98-39554
979.4'61—dc21                                     CIP

Printed in Singapore.

Cover and interior illustrations by Joe VanDerBos
Designed by Pete Friedrich at Charette Communication Design

Distributed in Canada by Raincoast Books
9050 Shaughnessy Street
Vancouver, British Columbia V6P 6E5

10 9 8 7 6 5 4 3

Chronicle Books
680 Second Street
San Francisco, California 94107

www.chroniclebooks.com

## INTRODUCTION

San Francisco is often called America's favorite city, and with good reason.

The city boasts panoramic hills so steep you can lean against them, cable cars, fog swirling around the Golden Gate Bridge, Chinatown, and Alcatraz looming in the bay.

Beginning with the Gold Rush, San Francisco has beckoned people from all over the world, giving the city both its multicultural heritage and its hedonistic "anything goes" reputation. "A heritage of the Wild West is still preserved in San Francisco," said Lawrence Davies in 1960. "It is shown in a willingness to engage in the experimental." It therefore comes as no surprise that the Beat Generation, the hippie "Flower Power" revolution, gay liberation, and yuppie narcissism took root here. San Franciscans seldom engage in the conventional or the expected. "It is perfectly common," wrote Richard Atcheson in 1970, "for a middle-aged Pacific Heights matron to abandon her beige-and-white drawing room for an afternoon on the barricades at Berkeley or San Francisco State, having made careful arrangements for bail in advance."

*Surrounded by water on three sides, the city charms visitors with its astonishing views, quaint Victorian houses, and unusual climate.*

The constant threat of earthquakes, one of which nearly annihilated
the city in 1906, also contributes to San Francisco's "live for today" philosophy. Children are
brought up with the understanding that it's only a matter of
time before the next one strikes, and earthquake safety drills are
common. "Because of our wooden houses and memories of 1906,"
said Herb Caen, "firecrackers are forbidden except as a religious
observance in Chinatown. Hence, the only time a young
San Francisco boy can celebrate the Fourth of July in the
American tradition is on the Chinese New Year."

*People here take pride in the statement "only in San Francisco."*

People here take pride in the statement "only in San
Francisco." Only in San Francisco would city planners
have the vision to span the Golden Gate with the world's
most spectacular bridge, to build the country's first sub-
way in over a half-century, and to make a pyramid-shaped building
the centerpiece of the downtown skyline even as they preserved its
obsolete cable cars. It is a city that is at once elegant, glamorous,
witty, absurd, tawdry, and deviant, giving San Francisco a mystique

all its own. "Somehow the great cities of America have taken their places in a mythology that shapes their destiny," wrote Joe Flower in 1979. "Money lives in New York. Power sits in Washington. Freedom sips cappuccino in a sidewalk cafe in San Francisco."

*San Francisco Secrets* takes a look at unusual and little-known facts of America's most-visited city, separating myth from reality and focusing not only on the hidden history of the city's favorite landmarks but on those frequently bypassed by tourists and unknown even to lifelong residents.

## ALAMO SQUARE

It is believed that some San Franciscans who died in the 1906 earthquake and fire are buried in Alamo Square. A temporary camp was almost set up in the square for those left homeless by the 1989 Loma Prieta earthquake. The terrace of restored three-story wooden homes on the east side of Steiner Street between Hayes and Fulton Streets across from Alamo Square was built by Irish-born property developer Matthew Kavanaugh in the 1890s. They were originally sold for $3,500. Kavanaugh, who lived at 722 Steiner from 1892 through 1900, couldn't have envisioned that a century later his houses would be among the most photographed vantage points in San Francisco, known as "postcard row." The colorfully painted, elaborate Victorians contrast sharply with the skyscrapers of the Financial District looming in the background. The houses have been the "homes" of characters in the motion pictures *Invasion of the Body Snatchers* (1978), *The Woman in Red* (1984), and *Maxie* (1985), and the television programs *Too Close for Comfort* (1980–86) and *Full House* (1987–95).

*Refugees from the 1906 earthquake and fire lived on the hill until their homes were rebuilt.*

## ALCATRAZ ISLAND

The rock island with its stark prison was the home of such infamous criminals as Al Capone, Machine Gun Kelly, and Robert "the Birdman of Alcatraz" Stroud. Surrounded by 1.5 miles of frigid water, the "Rock" was deemed "escape proof," though 36 tried in 14 separate attempts. There is no evidence that any of the escapes were successful. Five prisoners were never found and presumed dead. The prison closed in 1963, and tourists were allowed to visit the island beginning in 1973. The first lighthouse on the West Coast was installed there in 1854. Four years later the island became an army fortification, and military prisoners were kept there as early as 1861. Alcatraz became a federal maximum security prison in 1934. A few buildings, including the Warden's House, were destroyed during the Native American occupation of Alcatraz in 1969. The group claimed the island as part of an 1868 federal treaty with the Sioux nation that granted it any "unused government land."

*The island has no natural water or vegetation. Water and top-soil had to be shipped from the mainland.*

## ALTA PLAZA PARK

Alta Plaza Park, located atop Pacific Heights between Jackson, Clay, Scott, and Steiner Streets, has terraces sloping down to Clay Street. Some believe the terraces are a landing platform for spacecraft. The park offers views of the Western Addition, St. Mary's Cathedral, Marin County, Twin Peaks, and the Civic Center. Ryan O'Neal and Barbra Streisand were involved in a car chase down the stairs of the park in the 1972 movie *What's Up Doc?* Director Peter Bogdanovich ordered take after take of the scene, and the vehicles put an abundance of chips and cracks in the stairs. The film company enraged city officials by refusing to repair the fissures, which are still visible.

*The park's south stairway reproduces the grand stairway of the casino at Monte Carlo.*

## ANCHOR STEAM BEER

The forty-niners desired a cold brew, but everything necessary for the brewing of beer, even the ice, had to be shipped from the East around Cape Horn. It was simply too expensive to brew conventional beer. Enterprising San Franciscans invented steam beer, which fermented naturally in the cool climate. The lager is the only beer native to the United States and, until the opening of the transcontinental railroad in 1869, was the only beer available in San Francisco. At one time, there were 27 steam breweries operating in San Francisco, but only Anchor Steam, which began operation in 1851, survived Prohibition. Near bankruptcy in 1965, the Anchor Steam Brewery was saved by Stanford University student Fritz Maytag, whose family had earlier reaped a fortune with a different kind of suds: manufacturing washing machines in Iowa. The brewery is located at 1705 Mariposa Street in Potrero Hill.

*San Francisco's steam beer had its origins in the Gold Rush.*

## ANGEL ISLAND

The largest island in San Francisco Bay—rising to the summit of Mount Livermore at 781 feet above sea level—served early whalers as an anchorage and for replenishing supplies of food and water. Spanish naval lieutenant Juan Manuel de Ayala anchored there in 1775 during the first European expedition to sail into San Francisco Bay. The island was reserved for military purposes by President Millard Fillmore in 1850. Camp Reynolds was built there in 1863 as a fortification, followed by Fort McDowell in 1900. The army retained a presence until 1946. The island was also used as a prison for Native Americans, a quarantine station for smallpox victims, a detention center for enemy aliens during World War I, an internment camp for Italian and German prisoners during World War II, and a debarkation point for soldiers during the Spanish-American War and the two World Wars. From 1909 to 1940, Angel Island was the "Ellis Island of the West," serving mostly Asian immigrants. Dozens of faded Chinese poems are still inscribed on the walls of the barracks that served as a holding area for immigrants awaiting their citizen papers.

*During the 1950s and 1960s, Angel Island was an active Nike missile base.*

## AQUATIC PARK

Aquatic Park at the foot of Hyde Street contains a quarter-mile sandy beach and a large terraced lawn. It is one of the last remaining stretches of open shoreline along the northern waterfront. The curving 1,850-foot-long Municipal Pier is a popular spot for fishing and shelters the waters of the park. Sand was trucked in for the beach when the park was created as part of a WPA project in 1937. During World War II, the park was reserved for military personnel only. It was returned to the public after the war. Most people consider the waters of the San Francisco Bay too cold for swimming, but members of the Dolphin Club and South End Rowing Club brave the frigid currents every day. In the late 19th century, this was one of San Francisco's industrial districts and the waterfront was scarred with railways. Stonework from an abandoned 19th-century cemetery was used to build the seawall at the park.

*Tons of debris were dumped in the vicinity after the 1906 earthquake and fire. Much of it is still visible.*

## ASIAN ART MUSEUM

The Asian Art Museum in Golden Gate Park opened in 1966 after Chicagoan and millionaire businessman Avery Brundage donated his world-famous collection of Asian art to San Francisco "to bridge the gap between the East and West." He represented the United States in the decathlon at the 1912 Olympics and for many years was president of the International Olympic Committee. Brundage began his collection in 1936 after becoming fascinated by Asian cultures during his extensive travels with the Olympics. The collection, which is rotated periodically, contains nearly 10,000 paintings, sculptures, ceramics, jade objects, and textiles. The pieces cover 6,000 years of the history of some 40 countries. The Asian Art Museum will move to the renovated old San Francisco Main Library building at Larkin and McAllister Streets.

*Only about 15 percent of the Asian Art Museum's extensive collection is on display at any one time.*

### AUDIFFRED BUILDING

The Audiffred Building was erected in 1889 at Mission and Steuart Streets by Hippolite d'Audiffred, a Parisian who reached San Francisco by way of Veracruz, Mexico, having escaped Mexico's anti-Maximilian revolt. Originally a warehouse on what was then the waterfront, the building became the first headquarters of the first seaman's union in the world. Audiffred made a fortune selling charcoal to the Chinese, who needed the fuel to run their laundries. He saved his structure from the 1906 fire by bribing firemen with free whiskey and wine secured from the Bulkhead Saloon located in the building. It was the only downtown building on the south waterfront to survive the blaze. The Audiffred Building was gutted in a 1980 fire and has since been restored.

*The Audiffred Building reflects a style typical of the Champs Elysées in Paris.*

## BAKER BEACH

The 95,000-pound cannon placed behind Baker Beach is a replica of a defensive gun battery once located on the site. The original was deemed obsolete and sold for scrap after World War II. The replacement cannon was installed in 1977. The World War II bunkers are still visible. One of the most popular beaches in the city, the mile-long sandy shore of Baker Beach is located at the end of Bowley Street off Lincoln Avenue in the southwest corner of the Presidio. High dunes protect it from the coldest winds, and the beach is fringed by rocky cliffs and strands of cypress and pine trees, many of which were planted to conceal the gun emplacements. The southern end of Baker Beach is popular with families. The northern end, which offers a more dramatic view of the Golden Gate Bridge, attracts devotees of nude sunbathing. The large waves, currents, and cold water make the beach a dangerous place for swimming.

*Battery Chamberlain, a defensive fortification begun in 1904, was located on the site.*

### BALMY ALLEY

Balmy Alley, off 24th Street between Treat and Harrison Streets, was the site of the Mission District's first community mural, painted in 1973. It's been said the alley has the largest number of murals per square foot than anywhere in the world. The vivid pictures adorn nearly every wall surface. They were originally painted by schoolchildren and were continued by an affiliation of local artists. Some of the murals are decorative; others make powerful political statements. The predominant themes are peace in Central America, community pride, and AIDS awareness. The murals were dedicated in 1984 with a parade down Balmy Alley. Prominent murals in the Mission District are also located at 22nd Street and South Van Ness Avenue and at the entrance to the BART station at 24th and Mission.

*In the Mission District, murals decorate everything from restaurants to banks to schools to garage doors.*

## BANK OF AMERICA

With the use of special effects, 86 floors were added to the high-rise Bank of America headquarters building to make it the tallest in the world for use in the disaster film *The Towering Inferno*. Completed in 1971 and occupying the block bounded by California, Kearny, Pine, and Montgomery Streets, the Bank of America high-rise is clad in South Dakota carnelian granite. The building was controversial because the color contrasted sharply with the mostly white San Francisco skyline. In the evening, the reflecting rays of the setting sun cause the red exterior to gleam brightly. At 779 feet, it is the second tallest building in the city. Its 2 million square feet of office space make it the city's largest. The abstract 200-ton black polished Swedish-granite sculpture on the plaza is officially called *Transcendence*, but is irreverently known as the "Banker's Heart." The Bank of America was founded by Genoa-born A. P. Gianinni in 1904 as the Bank of Italy. During the 1906 fire, he carried the bank's assets out of town in a wagon under a load of vegetables. It was renamed the Bank of America in 1930.

*The headquarters building of the Bank of America was the model for the edifice that burned in the 1974 disaster flick The Towering Inferno.*

## BARBARY COAST

The once notorious Barbary Coast, named for the pirate hideout in North Africa, was located in an area bounded by Broadway, Embarcadero, Grant, and Washington. Many cities had red-light districts with unsavory reputations, but none seemed to approach the Barbary Coast, which set standards for unbridled wickedness and depravity. The streets were thick with brothels, bars, gambling, and opium dens. There was all manner of "entertainment," including Oofty Goofty, who let people hit him across the backside with a baseball bat for 50 cents, until he was crippled by boxer John L. Sullivan. It was here the terms *shanghai, hoodlum,* and *Mickey Finn* originated. As many as 23 kidnap gangs operated in the city in 1852, making huge profits by drugging unsuspecting seamen, who were then put into involuntary servitude on undermanned ships set to sail to faraway ports. The Barbary Coast thrived from the 1850s until it was finally shut down in 1917, when a federal decree closed the brothels. The area, now gentrified, is known as Jackson Square.

*During the heyday of the Barbary Coast, the junction of Jackson and Kearny Streets was known as "Murderer's Corner."*

## BART

The BART system's transbay tube, which rests on the bay floor 130 feet below the surface, sits in the soft mud and away from rock because of the threat from earthquakes. BART's 71-mile elevated, surface, and underground system opened in 1972. It takes passengers from San Francisco to the East Bay and south of the city to Colma and Daly City in sleek air-conditioned trains that travel up to 80 miles per hour. When originally conceived in the early 1950s, BART was slated to run through nine counties, but was eventually whittled to three (San Francisco, Contra Costa, and Alameda). San Mateo County withdrew because local merchants feared BART would siphon shopping traffic to San Francisco. Marin County dropped out when the Golden Gate Bridge authority refused to allow tracks to run across the span. BART planners wanted to add a deck under the existing bridge roadway for the trains.

*The underground tube built by the Bay Area Rapid Transit under the bay from San Francisco to Oakland is 3.6 miles long.*

## BAY TO
## BREAKERS RACE

From its modest beginnings, the
Bay to Breakers grew to attract 20,000
by the 1970s, and by the 1980s the race
reached its peak participation of 100,000. About
75,000 participate today. Held the third Sunday in May, the
*San Francisco Examiner* Bay to Breakers is more than a 7.5 mile
race. It's also a parade attended by 100,000 people and a testimony

*Known origi-
nally as the
Cross City Race,
the Bay to
Breakers began
in 1912 and
never drew more
than 125 runners
until 1965.*

to the fitness consciousness and lively sense of the absurd
characteristic of San Francisco. The race begins at the foot
of Howard Street, winds through downtown, climbs the
Hayes Street hill, and traverses Golden Gate Park to Ocean
Beach. The race is for serious runners, but most of those
who run come to have a good time and run in every kind
of costume imaginable including airplanes, jukeboxes, and
buildings, or in three-piece suits carrying briefcases. Some
run in tandem in getups such as centipedes or huge con-
doms. A few run totally nude except for shoes and socks.
Women were not officially permitted to compete in the
race until 1971.

## BEATLES'
## LAST CONCERT

The concert took place at Candlestick Park on August 29, 1966, before an audience of 25,000 in the 45,000-seat capacity stadium. The Fab Four performed on a temporary stage in the infield surrounded by a six-foot fence. The master of ceremonies was Gene Nelson, one of the leading DJs of KYA-AM. They played for 33 minutes starting at 9:27 P.M. following the support acts of the Cyrkle and the Ronnetts. The Beatles began their final concert with "Rock and Roll Music" and ended with "Long Tall Sally." Although the Beatles continued recording together until 1970, they did not play live in concert after 1966 because of the frenzy and noise of the crowds. The Beatles also played in the Bay Area at the Cow Palace in Daly City on August 19, 1964, their first concert on their first American tour, and again with two shows at the same venue in 1965.

*The Beatles made their last live appearance in San Francisco.*

## BIRDMAN
## OF ALCATRAZ

Robert Stroud, who spent his last 54 years in prison for two murders, was an internationally known authority on birds and published a 60,000-word manuscript on bird diseases that was regarded as a classic in its field. Stroud's interest in birds began in 1920 at the federal prison in Leavenworth, Kansas, when he found a nest in a prison yard underneath a branch that fell during a storm. Stroud nursed the four baby sparrows back to health. Eventually he had over 300 birds in cages he built from cigar boxes and studied bird lore 20 hours a day. Stroud was transferred to Alcatraz in 1942, but was not allowed to keep birds there. He became known as the Birdman of Alcatraz because of a 1955 biography with that title and a 1962 movie based on his life. Stroud was far from the mild-mannered man portrayed in the film by Burt Lancaster, however. He died in 1973 at the age of 73.

*Robert Stroud, known as the Birdman of Alcatraz, never kept birds at the famous prison.*

## BIRTHPLACE OF
## THE UNITED NATIONS

There was considerable sentiment to keep the U.N. in San Francisco, where it began, but it was moved to New York City because many European nations believed San Francisco was too far to travel. The opening sessions of the United Nations were held at the War Memorial Opera House at Van Ness Avenue and Grove Street in the Civic Center beginning in April 1945. High-level diplomats met at the Fairmont Hotel to discuss details of the peace-keeping organization. On June 26, 1945, during the waning days of World War II, representatives of 50 nations signed the U.N. charter next door to the Opera House at the Herbst Theater. The United Nations Plaza at Market and Hyde

*San Francisco was the birth-place of the United Nations.*

Streets commemorates the event. The Fairmont Hotel flies the flags of each of the countries of the United Nations above its main entrance. The formal peace treaty between the United States and Japan was also signed at the War Memorial Opera House, in 1951.

## BLACK BART'S
## HANDKERCHIEF

Charles Boles, also known as
Charles Bolton but better known as
Black Bart, gained fame by single-handedly
holding up 28 stagecoaches on the lonesome roads
of Northern California between 1875 and 1883 without
firing a shot. The famous highwayman often left behind humor-
ous mocking poems. At the scene of his last holdup, Black Bart
mistakenly dropped a handkerchief with a distinctive
laundry mark. Wells Fargo detective Harry Morse traced it
to a laundry on Bush Street in San Francisco, then tracked
down Black Bart and arrested him. Black Bart turned out
to be a dapper, mild-mannered mining engineer. He was
about 50 years old when he committed his last robbery.
Boles served five years at San Quentin prison, then disap-
peared, never to be heard from again. Some believe he
turned once again to robbing stagecoaches. There is a display devoted to the infamous bandit at the Wells Fargo
History Museum in the Wells Fargo Bank Building at
Montgomery and Sacramento Streets.

*The infamous bandit Black Bart's patronage of a San Francisco laundry led to his arrest.*

## BOHEMIAN CLUB

The Bohemian Club was organized in 1072 by a group of journalists, writers, and painters. In the early days, the membership was truly bohemian, including Ambrose Bierce, John Muir, Bret Harte, Joaquin Miller, Jack London, Sinclair Lewis, and George Sterling. Sterling, who wrote 18 volumes of poetry, committed suicide in his room at the club in 1926. Today, the Bohemian Club is a male-only enclave of businessmen and industrialists. The building at Taylor and Post Streets, erected in 1934, is red brick and covered in ivy. The basement contains a theater, and the club maintains downtown's only boxwood hedge. It is one of a dozen exclusive clubs located just northwest of Union Square at the foot of Nob Hill. Bohemian Grove, the club's 2,700-acre summer retreat north of the city on the Russian River, draws the rich and famous, including presidents, cabinet members, and movie stars.

*The bronze cornerstone owl on the Bohemian Club is emblazoned with the motto "Weaving spiders come not here."*

## BROADWAY

The section of Broadway between Columbus Avenue and Montgomery Street has been a center of San Francisco's nightlife since the Barbary Coast days of the late 1800s and early 1900s. In the 1930s, it was a center for bootlegging. In the 1950s, comedy and folk clubs like the Purple Onion and hungry i proliferated. Lenny Bruce, Bill Cosby, Richard Pryor, Woody Allen, Barbra Streisand, Mort Sahl, Dick Gregory, the Smothers Brothers, Phyllis Diller, and Johnny Mathis were among the entertainers who performed on the street early in their careers. Beginning in 1964, topless strip clubs began to line the avenue, peaking in the early 1970s. By the 1980s, the advent of VCRs, with cheap porn available on tape, led to the decline of the strip clubs. Many of the old Broadway clubs have become restaurants.

*Broadway is wider than most San Francisco streets because it was the principal route to the docks.*

## BUBONIC PLAGUE

The bubonic plague invaded San Francisco in 1900, arriving via infected rats on sailing ships from Asia. The death toll in San Francisco was 113, almost all confined to Chinatown, before the disease appeared to be eradicated. A banquet was held at the St. Francis Hotel on March 18, 1905, to celebrate the end of the epidemic, but it proved to be premature. In 1907, the Black Death surfaced again in Chinatown, killing another 77. The city decided that the most effective means of combating the problem was to rid the city of rats, the principal carriers of the plague. Individuals were paid 10 cents for every rat that was taken to the health department. More than 150,000 rats were captured, 11,200 buildings were disinfected, and 1,713 structures were demolished.

*The Black Death has had two outbreaks in modern-day San Francisco.*

## BUDDHA'S
## UNIVERSAL TEMPLE

The largest Buddhist temple in the United States, Buddha's Universal Temple is located on the corner of Washington and Kearny Streets in Chinatown. The congregation of the temple is a member of the Pristine Orthodox Dharma, a strongly Americanized modern offshoot of Buddhism. Once the site of a nightclub, the building was purchased by church members in 1951 for $500, only to be condemned by the city as structurally unsound. Volunteers worked to rebuild it entirely by hand using a variety of polished exotic woods, and the temple was dedicated in 1963. On the roof is a lotus pool and a Bodhi tree, said to be a shoot from a tree under which the Buddha arrived at enlightenment more than 2,500 years ago.

*Much of the money for the temple's construction was raised by fortune cookie sales.*

## CABLE CAR
## BELL-RINGING
## CONTEST

In the contest, conductors give a one-minute "concert" and are judged for rhythm, flair, loudness, and musicality. The bells carried by the cable car conductors and gripmen date from 1882 and are used as a system of communication between the two. Three rings of a bell, for instance, means an emergency stop is necessary. Originally, the city required all conductors to carry bells or gongs and ring them as they crossed intersections because there were no traffic signals. A cable car gripman starts and stops the car by gripping the two-inch moving cable—set 27 inches deep in the center of the street—to make the car go forward and releasing it to stop the car, as if with a giant pair of pliers. When the grip is fully activated, the gripman is in a nearly horizontal position. It is a physically demanding job, and the attrition rate is high during the training period. It takes great skill, especially where the lines cross and the cars "ride free," unattached to the cable. Tension has to be adjusted constantly to keep the bale from slipping. Rib, knee, hand, and back injuries are common. The conductor applies the rear wheel and track brakes.

*Every summer, a bell-ringing contest takes place on Union Square.*

## CALIFORNIA ACADEMY OF SCIENCES

The oldest scientific institution in the West, the California Academy of Sciences was founded in 1853 by a small group of naturalists who held weekly meetings and published papers on the state's newly discovered species. Most of the academy's holdings, then at 833 Market Street, were destroyed in the 1906 fire. Much was saved, however, by Alice Eastwood, the academy's curator of botany, at great risk to her own life. She continued at her job until 1953, when she died at the age of 94. The academy has been located in Golden Gate Park since 1916. It incorporates the Steinhart Aquarium, the Natural History Museum, and the Morrison Planetarium. The planetarium's laserium features laser-light shows choreographed to music. The Space and Earth Hall includes an "earthquake floor" that enables visitors to ride a simulated California earthquake. The totem pole in the courtyard was built by the Canadian Native American group Gitksan, which calls itself Ksan for short. Noting a similarity to its call letters, radio station KSAN brought the tribe to San Francisco during the 1970s to erect the totem.

*The Whale Fountain in the courtyard was made for the 1939 World's Fair on Treasure Island.*

## CALIFORNIA PALACE OF THE LEGION OF HONOR

The Palace of the Legion of Honor is a replica of the French pavilion of the 1915 Panama-Pacific International Exposition. The pavilion in turn was a copy of the Palais de la Legion d'Honneur in Paris. The gift of Adolph and Alma de Bretteville Spreckels to the city, the California Palace of the Legion of Honor is San Francisco's repository for European art. It stands amid the Monterey pines and cypresses of Lincoln Park and commands a broad view of the city from its hilltop site. The museum was dedicated on Armistice Day in 1924 to the 3,600 Californians who died during World War I. It features a world-class collection of painting, sculpture, decorative arts, and works on paper, illustrating the development of European art from the medieval period through the beginning of the 20th century. There are more than 100 statues by Rodin at the museum. George Segal's haunting sculpture *The Holocaust,* with emaciated corpses and a solitary figure peering through barbed wire, is a shocking reminder of the World War II horror.

*The courtyard contains one of the five original bronze castings of Rodin's The Thinker.*

## THE CANNERY

The Cannery was empty for 30 years until it was remodeled into a shopping center in 1968. Originally constructed in 1909 for the Del Monte Fruit Company, and located on Leavenworth and Jefferson Streets, the Cannery contains shops, restaurants, a comedy club, galleries, and a movie theater. Arched windows preserve its Victorian past. The interior reveals a seamless design of open stairwells, bridges, spacious courtyards, and passageways. Treasures from the estate of William Randolph Hearst have been installed in some of the facilities. In Jack's Bar on the ground floor are a Jacobean carved fireplace, a plaster ceiling, and oak paneling dating from 1609. In the courtyard is a century-old grove of olive trees. The Museum of the City of San Francisco, opened in 1991, is located on the third floor.

*The most productive peach-canning operation in the world was in the Cannery from 1916 through 1937.*

## CASTRO DISTRICT

The center of San Francisco's gay social life, the Castro District is a collection of unique shops, bars, restaurants, and restored Victorians on the streets of Eureka Valley at the base of Twin Peaks, bounded roughly by 16th, 22nd, Douglass, and Dolores Streets. Rainbow flags symbolizing gay pride adorn the windows of homes and businesses. Beginning in the early 1970s, the Castro, as it is now called, saw the mass arrival of gay men and women. No one knows how many gays and lesbians now reside in San Francisco, but it is estimated to be at least 100,000 in a city of 725,000. San Francisco's gay community has its roots in the Gold Rush, when the emerging city consisted mostly of young males. Newspapers of the day told of the exploits of the "Lavender Cowboys." Military purges of homosexuals during World War II had a profound effect on making San Francisco a destination of gays. Those serving in the South Pacific were dismissed to the port of San Francisco, and many opted to stay.

*Up until the 1960s, the world's most famous gay neighborhood was a mostly Irish Catholic neighborhood known as the Most Holy Redeemer Parish.*

## CASTRO THEATER

The 1922 Spanish Baroque Castro Theater at 429 Castro Street, designed by Timothy Pflueger, presents one of the best repertory movie schedules in the city. The giant, vertical, pink-and-blue neon sign was added in 1937. The original Wurlitzer pipe organ is still played. As it slowly rises from the orchestra pit, the organist breaks into the song "San Francisco" just before the feature. The Castro seats 1,600 and has avoided the fate of most neighborhood theaters, which have been divided into smaller theaters or have passed into oblivion. It was declared a Historic Landmark in 1977. The ceiling, the main feature of the unaltered, ornate Arabian Nights interior, is cast in plaster to resemble a giant cloth canopy tent with swags, ropes, and tassels. The San Francisco Gay and Lesbian Film Festival is held at the theater each June.

*The Castro Theater is the last remaining 1920s movie palace in San Francisco that is still showing films.*

## CHILDREN'S FOUNTAIN

San Francisco's history is portrayed in a unique manner in the Ruth Asawa Fountain on the Grand Hyatt Hotel on Stockton Street at Union Square. The bronze relief, completed in 1972, is made up of 41 plaques that cover the circular wall of the fountain in maplike fashion. Thousands of sculpted figures on the plaques depict different aspects of the city. Some 250 citizens of San Francisco, from ages three to 90, helped Asawa shape figures that meld reality, myth, and fantasy, the latter exemplified by Superman flying over Montgomery Street. The relief was modeled from bread dough before being cast in metal. Asawa also designed the mermaid fountain at Ghirardelli Square.

*Children helped sculptor Ruth Asawa design the fountain's figures.*

## CHINA BEACH

Also known as Phelan Beach, China Beach was named for the Chinese fishermen who used to camp in the area in the 1870s. Later, when government restrictions stopped immigration from China, it is believed that people were smuggled into San Francisco here. Earlier, it was the westernmost point on the Underground Railroad, which spirited escaped slaves out of the South. In the 1920s, there was a long wrangle over the property, as residents of the exclusive Sea Cliff neighborhood desired to keep the beach in private hands. Most San Franciscans wanted the beach open to the public, however, and the state and the city purchased it for $160,000 in 1933. At the east end of the beach are submerged granite paving stones dumped after the 1906 earthquake. They have been polished smooth by nearly a century of relentless waves and tides. Many weddings are staged at this spot. Sea Cliff, with dramatic views of the Golden Gate, is the only San Francisco neighborhood that touches the ocean. Actor Robin Williams is among those who live here.

*China Beach is one of the few beaches in San Francisco where lifeguards are on duty and swimming is considered safe, although still cold.*

## CHINATOWN

Chinese immigrants first settled near Portsmouth Square, the city's historic center, at the time of the Gold Rush. Chinatown has been located in the same area for 150 years, and unlike the rest of the city's ethnic communities, it has not moved, only expanded. Although Chinatown is roughly bounded by Broadway, Powell, Kearny, and Bush Streets, residential Chinatown extends well into North Beach, the result of a new wave of immigration from China and Southeast Asia beginning in the 1970s. After the 1906 earthquake and fire destroyed the community, developers and politicians planned to relocate the Chinese to less desirable property at Hunter's Point. The resident population rebuilt quickly, however, before City Hall could act. The Stockton Street Tunnel, completed in 1914 between Bush and Sacramento Streets, originally had tunnels that extended into the basements of Chinatown buildings to provide an escape in case of an earthquake. The tunnels are no longer maintained, however.

*Due to restrictive clauses in real estate contracts, the Chinese were unable to buy property outside of Chinatown until 1948.*

## CHINATOWN GATEWAY

The ornate three-arch gateway over Grant Avenue at Bush Street marks the southern entrance to Chinatown. The design of the dragon-studded gate is based on the ceremonial entrances traditional in Chinese villages, and its three green-tiled roofs are topped by various good luck symbols. The portal is guarded by stone lion dogs, mythical creatures that are supposed to give protection against evil spirits. The dolphins along the roof edge symbolize prosperity. Chinese characters above the gate read: "All Under Heaven is Good for the People." It is also known as the "Dragon's Gate." The dragon streetlights along Grant Avenue were installed much earlier, in 1925, about the time that Chinatown became a tourist attraction. The Chinese ornamentation on buildings throughout Chinatown began to appear at the same time.

*Erected in 1970, the Chinatown Gateway was a gift from Taiwan.*

## CHINESE SIX COMPANIES

Formally known as the Chinese Consolidated Benevolent Association and founded in 1862, the Chinese Six Companies are headquartered at 843 Stockton Street. The organization was founded to combat discrimination and give the immigrants a sense of identity in their new homeland. The 1909 building, splashed with bright yellow, red, green, and blue, is one of the most elaborate and colorful in Chinatown. In the 19th century, the organization recruited Chinese laborers to work on the transcontinental railroad. The Chinese word *ku li,* which translates to "bitter toil," became the English word *coolie.* It also functioned as an unofficial governing body to settle disputes, operate Chinese schools, control importation of goods from China, care for the sick, provide legal services, and witness contracts and property sales, not only within Chinatown but nationwide. Although the association has lost much of its former prestige, it still wields important social power.

*The Chinese Six Companies touched many aspects of life in the Chinese community.*

## CHURCH OF JOHN COLTRANE

Jazz lovers flock from all over the world to the storefront church at 351 Divisadero Street in the Western Addition to hear the house band Ohnedaruth play Coltrane's music every Sunday. The band's name derives from the Sanskrit word for compassion and is the spiritual name Alice Coltrane gave her husband when he died. Those who bring musical instruments are encouraged to sit in with the band. The four-hour service is presided over by a bishop who founded the church, formally known as St. John's African Orthodox Church, while undergoing a religious experience after attending one of Coltrane's live appearances.

*The Church of John Coltrane has used his music for divine liturgy since 1974.*

## CITY HALL

The original City Hall structure, completed in 1898 at McAllister and Larkin Streets, collapsed in a heap during the 1906 earthquake. The focal point of the Civic Center, the current City Hall, was designed by John Bakewell and Arthur Brown. This 1915 building covers two city blocks bounded by Polk, McAllister, Van Ness, and Grove. The huge lead-lined, green copper dome is modeled after St. Peter's Basilica in Rome and dominates the area, rising 301 feet above the street, higher than the Capitol dome in Washington, D.C. The building, 400 feet long and 300 feet wide, has an exterior of granite from the foothills of the Sierra Nevada. In 1960, civil rights and freedom-of-speech protesters were washed down the central stairway with fire hoses. Mayor Dianne Feinstein was married at City Hall in 1980 and invited the entire city to her wedding reception. In 1991, dozens of gay couples were married on the front steps. Badly damaged by the 1989 earthquake, City Hall's arches were supported by large wooden struts until the building was closed in 1995 for seismic retrofitting.

*San Francisco's previous City Hall was built of inferior materials, including trash and newspaper, by a corrupt city administration.*

## CITY LIGHTS BOOKSTORE

Opened in 1953, City Lights Bookstore at 261 Columbus Avenue in North Beach was one of the nation's first all-paperback bookstores and the de facto headquarters of the Beat Generation, which emerged in the 1950s and put North Beach on the map. It is testament to the long-standing influence of the Beats. From its beginnings to the present day, City Lights owner Lawrence Ferlinghetti has published and sold alternative forms of literature. He gained national notoriety in 1956 when he published Allen Ginsberg's incendiary, apocalyptic poem *Howl* and was arrested for obscenity. Ferlinghetti and Ginsberg won the landmark case. City Lights appeared in the 1981 movie *Heart Beat*, starring Nick Nolte and Sissy Spacek, which detailed the relationship of Beats Jack Kerouac and Neal Cassidy. It was also in the 1990 film *Flashback* featuring Dennis Hopper as a 1960s radical autographing his autobiography in the store.

*The bookstore was named for the 1931 Charlie Chaplin film of the same name.*

## CIVIC CENTER

At the time of the 1906 earthquake, San Francisco was the largest city in the country west of St. Louis, a distinction it would lose to Los Angeles by 1920. San Francisco's Civic Center was designed to reflect the city's stature. Begun in 1912 and located in the triangle between Market Street and Van Ness and Golden Gate Avenues, it is acclaimed as the finest example of Beaux Arts architecture in the United States. Beaux Arts was a movement initiated by young American architects who were inspired by classical architecture. The Civic Auditorium, one of the buildings in the complex, hosted the 1920 Democratic Party national convention, which nominated James Cox for president. Cox lost the election to Warren Harding. Ironically, Harding died in San Francisco in 1923. The War Memorial Opera House, built in 1932, was the first city-owned opera house in the country and is the home of the San Francisco Ballet. Established in 1933, it is America's oldest resident classical ballet company.

*The Civic Center's grand plan was designed shortly after the 1906 earthquake and fire to show the world that the city had recovered.*

## CLIFF HOUSE

The Cliff House, at Point Lobos Avenue and the Great Highway, was one of San Francisco's first tourist attractions. The present structure is the third Cliff House built on the site. The first, built in 1863, was originally the weekend resort for many of San Francisco's wealthiest citizens, but by the 1880s had degenerated into a haven for gamblers, drunks, and prostitutes. It was nearly destroyed in 1887 when a schooner carrying dynamite exploded just offshore. The building burned to the ground on Christmas Eve, 1894. The second version of the Cliff House, built by Adolph Sutro in 1896, catered to middle-class families and was by far the most impressive: a seven-story, flamboyant, Victorian building perched improbably on a headland above the crashing waves of the Pacific Ocean, with an observation tower 200 feet above sea level. It became a blazing ruin in a spectacular fire in 1907. The present-day utilitarian building, erected in 1909 and extensively remodeled, houses the Cliff House Restaurant.

*Presidents Rutherford B. Hayes, Ulysses S. Grant, William McKinley, Theodore Roosevelt, and William Howard Taft have visited the Cliff House.*

## COBWEB PALACE

The Cobweb Palace existed from 1856 through 1896 on Francisco Street between Powell and Mason. Its owner, Abe Warner, was superstitious about spiders and would never kill one or interfere with its work. After a while, cobwebs covered the walls and the ceilings. It was said that the webs were so thick they could support human weight. Warner also kept a miniature zoo in the place with bears, birds, kangaroos, and monkeys. Rather than turned off by the dingy, dirty, and gloomy atmosphere of the restaurant, San Franciscans flocked to the establishment. The quality of the food and drink was said to be unsurpassed, particularly the clam and crab dishes and the hot toddies.

*Spider webs covered everything in the 19th-century restaurant called the Cobweb Palace.*

## COIT
## MEMORIAL TOWER

Located at the top of Telegraph Hill, Coit Tower stands 210 feet tall. It was built in 1933 as a monument to firefighters with funds from the estate of Lillie Hitchcock Coit, who donated $125,000 "for the purpose of adding to the beauty of the city." Coit's lifelong fascination with fires began in 1851 at the age of seven when she was rescued by firefighters from a burning building in which two of her friends died. The daughter of a wealthy army surgeon, she rebelled against Victorian society and drew scowls from the straitlaced matrons of her day. She often dressed as a man to gamble in North Beach, played poker with dock workers, smoked cigars, sneaked away on a men's fishing trip, and was a Confederate sympathizer during the Civil War. Coit was made an honorary member of the Knickerbocker Hose Company No. 5 as a teenager, and her constant attendance at fires made her a local celebrity. For the rest of her life she was usually seen wearing the badge presented to her by the fire company, even at formal occasions. After she died, Lillie was cremated wearing the pin.

*Many believe the tower was built to resemble a fire nozzle, but historians insist this wasn't intentional.*

## COIT TOWER MURALS

Before the decision was reached to fill the space with murals, plans called for the ground floor of Coit Tower to house a restaurant or an exhibit hall. The murals by 25 local artists and their 19 assistants were created in the 1930s as part of the WPA project to alleviate the effects of the Great Depression on the artistic community and to decorate public buildings. They are painted in the "social realism" style of politically radical Mexican muralist Diego Rivera. The leftist style and content of some of the murals caused considerable controversy when they were unveiled, and delayed the opening of Coit Tower for several months while nervous authorities argued about the dangers of communism and socialism. The depictions of American labor during the 1930s were finished at a time when a bitter, violent longshoremen's strike rocked the city. The tower was closed briefly and a hammer and sickle were removed before the murals went to public view. The slogan "In God We Trust" was also removed from the "hammer and sickle" mural. The murals were restored in 1989.

*The murals, financed by the federal government, originally included the image of a hammer and sickle.*

## COLUMBUS AVENUE

Columbus Avenue was cut across the city's grid in 1872 from the Montgomery Block (now the site of the Transamerica Pyramid) downtown through North Beach to Fisherman's Wharf, then the city's industrial zone. The plan meant that many had to surrender a considerable amount of property for the right-of-way. The angle of the street through the valley between Russian and Telegraph Hills created a series of confusing five- and six-way intersections. Originally called Montgomery Avenue, it was changed to Columbus Avenue to honor North Beach's Italian population and has both English and Italian street signs. Many of the city's parades are held along Columbus Avenue.

*The platting of Columbus Avenue was highly controversial.*

## CONDOR CLUB

Carol Doda scandalously bared her silicone-enhanced 44-inch bustline and danced topless for the first time in 1964 at the Condor Club at Columbus Avenue and Broadway. For two decades Doda danced at the club, and her figure was displayed outside on a neon sign with blinking red lights for nipples. The sign was removed in 1991 (and auctioned off piecemeal). The club is now a cafe known as the Condor Bistro. Patrons can see Doda's old dressing room and a reproduction of the piano that, bearing Doda, ascended to the second floor at the end of her act. In 1983 the club manager had a late-night tryst with a waitress during which they accidentally activated the hydraulic apparatus. The two were crushed against the ceiling and the manager died in the mishap.

*The Condor Club claims that it started the strip joint craze for completely nude dancers.*

## CONSERVATORY
## OF FLOWERS

The conservatory is an elaborate Victorian building that houses a tropical garden, seasonal displays of flowers and plants, and a permanent exhibit of rare orchids. A copy of the Palm House at London's Kew Gardens, it is one of the largest conservatories in the United States, covering 15,000 square feet. The ornate greenhouse was originally brought around Cape Horn on a ship from Dublin, Ireland, in 1875 for the San Jose estate of James Lick. He died, however, before his greenhouse could be uncrated. Leland Stanford purchased the building and donated it to the park, where it was erected in 1879. The dome was destroyed in a fire in 1883 and rebuilt. It was one of several San Francisco locations featured in the 1993 movie *Heart and Souls*. The building was damaged extensively in a 1995 storm and is being restored.

*The Conservatory of Flowers is the oldest building in Golden Gate Park.*

## CONVENT OF
## THE SACRED HEART

The mansion at 2200 Broadway at Webster in Pacific Heights was constructed in 1910 for Joseph Grant, president of the Columbia Steel Company, who in 1920 helped to start the Save-the-Redwoods League. Since 1948, it has been the School of the Sacred Heart. The Flood mansion at 2222 Broadway was built soon after the 1906 earthquake and fire. After their Nob Hill manse was gutted in the disaster, James Leary Flood, whose father made a fortune in silver mining, promised his wife that he would build on granite. No granite existed in the area, so a granite base was imported at great expense. The mansion became the Convent of the Sacred Heart High School in 1940. The building at 2120 Broadway was erected by the Flood family in 1901 and now houses the Hamlin School for Girls. The mansion built by lumber and railroad magnate Andrew Hammond at 2252 Broadway in 1905 was converted to the Stuart School for Boys in 1956.

*The Convent of the Sacred Heart has preserved four of San Francisco's most imposing mansions by transforming them into private schools.*

## COW HOLLOW

In the 1860s, a small spring-fed lake near the present-day corner of Franklin and Lombard was called Washerwoman's Lagoon because women converged there to do their laundry. It was one of the few sources of fresh water in the city. In 1861, dairy farms began to appear, followed by tanneries, sausage factories, and slaughterhouses. The city prohibited livestock from the area by 1891 because of pollution and complaints about barnyard odors from residents of nearby Pacific Heights. The fetid lagoon was filled in by prisoners using sand from the dunes on Lombard Street. The fountain at St. Mary the Virgin Episcopal Church, built in 1891 at 2325 Union Street, is fed by one of the springs that meandered through the pastures of Cow Hollow's early dairies. The 1870 house and barn of dairyman James Cudworth still stands behind a palm tree at 2040 Union. Since the 1950s, Cow Hollow has undergone a remarkable transformation with the conversion of run-down Victorians into boutiques, art galleries, and cafes.

*The nine-block shopping district along Union Street between Van Ness and Steiner was named for the area's 30 dairy farms in the 1860s.*

### CROOKEDEST STREET

Although Lombard Street between Hyde and Leavenworth is advertised as the "crookedest street in the world," it's not even the crookedest in San Francisco. Lombard has eight turns in a space of 412 feet, while Vermont Street between 20th and 22nd Streets in Potrero Hill contains six turns in 270 feet. Lombard remains one of the city's top tourist attractions, however, because of its spectacular vistas atop Russian Hill. The views from Vermont Street are obscured by dense foliage. The colorful floral gardens of Lombard Street began in the 1940s when a resident of the street imported thousands of hydrangeas from France. The gardens are communally owned. The slalom descents that wind down Lombard and Vermont were designed in 1922 to make the streets more accessible to automobile traffic, like switchbacks on a mountain road. The turns reduced Lombard Street's grade from a natural 27 percent to 16 percent.

*Vermont Street is the crookedest street in San Francisco.*

## DASHIELL HAMMETT

Dashiell Hammett (1894–1961) was born in Connecticut and from 1920 through 1929 lived in San Francisco, where he wrote most of his crime novels featuring the detective Sam Spade. Before he gained fame by authoring *The Maltese Falcon,* Hammett worked as a detective for the Pinkerton Agency in San Francisco. Devoted readers have long retraced the steps of the characters in his novels. Spade lived on Post Street. The St. Francis Hotel is the model for the St. Mark in *The Maltese Falcon,* published in 1930. Spade's partner Miles Archer was shot in Burritt Alley, a tiny deadend street a block north of Union Square off Bush Street. Another significant Hammett location is John's Grill, his favorite restaurant, located at 63 Ellis Street, two blocks north of Union Square off Powell. Spade's office was in the Hunter-Dulin Building at 111 Sutter Street. Hammett finished the landmark work in apartment 2 at the San Loretto, 1155 Leavenworth Street, in Nob Hill. He also lived in several Tenderloin and Russian Hill apartments.

*Hammett's detective duties included working for the defense in the city's infamous Fatty Arbuckle case.*

## DENIM

Like many merchants during the Gold Rush, Levi Strauss journeyed to San Francisco to sell goods to the prospectors. An immigrant from Germany, he brought a load of canvas to turn into tents. Strauss had no success selling the tents, but constantly heard miners complain that their pants didn't hold up to the rigors of the gold mines. He turned the canvas into pants instead, and the garments were an instant hit. He eventually switched from canvas to a tough blue cotton fabric loomed in Nîmes, France, called *serge de Nîmes,* which quickly became the word "denim" and gave the trousers their trademark color. The name "jeans" came from the French word *Gênes* (meaning "Genoa"), as the trousers were reminiscent of those once worn by Genoan sailors. The copper rivets, originally designed for saddles, were added to reinforce the pants in the 1870s and emblazoned with the initials *SF* for San Francisco. Levi jeans became part of the popular culture during the 1950s, and business more than doubled during the 1960s. The company is still in San Francisco and is operated by descendants of Levi Strauss.

*Levi Strauss's original pants were brown in color and called waist-high overalls.*

## EARTHQUAKE OF 1989

The city's fireboat saved the Marina District from fiery destruction following the 1989 earthquake. During the 1980s, San Francisco had debated scrapping the city's only fireboat because it was seldom used and costly to maintain. After the earthquake, the city purchased a second fireboat. The quake's epicenter was in Loma Prieta in the sparsely populated Santa Cruz Mountains south of the city and produced 15 seconds of ferocious shaking. Eleven died within the city of San Francisco, most of them in the Marina District, the neighborhood that suffered the most damage. The relatively low loss of life throughout the Bay Area was credited to the World Series between the San Francisco Giants and Oakland Athletics. Fewer were on the roads than normal at that time of day because many San Franciscans were at home to watch the game. The quake irreparably damaged the Embarcadero Freeway, a double-decked elevated highway that aroused the ire of San Franciscans since it was erected in 1959 because it obscured the Ferry Building and views of the bay. It was dismantled in 1989.

*The earthquake of 1989 struck at 5:04 P.M. on October 17, registering 7.1 on the Richter scale.*

## EMBARCADERO

The Embarcadero, the Spanish word for "wharf" or "pier," is built on top of a seawall stretching six miles along San Francisco's waterfront from Fisherman's Wharf to China Basin. From the Gold Rush until the 1950s, the area was a beehive of activity, with freighters, steamships, schooners, whalers, and fishing boats loading and unloading cargo. Onshore saloons, cheap rooming houses, gambling halls, and cafes catered to sailors and longshoremen. Virtually all of the modern container shipping industry is gone, lost to the ports of Oakland and Long Beach. Many of the abandoned wharves have been razed for new development. The gentrification has brought apartments, restaurants, offices, parks, and walkways, along with a new ballpark in China Basin for the Giants baseball team. The Mechanics Monument at Market and Battery Streets, which pays tribute to waterfront mechanics, was dedicated in 1894 to the memory of Peter Donahue, owner of the city's first iron foundry, street railway, and gas company. The sculptor was Douglas Tilden, who was deaf and mute.

*The piers along the Embarcadero bear odd numbers north of the Ferry Building, even numbers south of the building.*

## EXPLORATORIUM

The founder of the Exploratorium was physicist Frank Oppenheimer, who worked on the development of the atomic bomb. His brother Robert, who worked with him in Los Alamos, New Mexico, during World War II, organized the scientific end of the project. Opened in 1969 and located in the cavernous, half-moon-shaped structure behind the Palace of Fine Arts rotunda, the Exploratorium is an innovative museum of science with some 650 exhibits based on hands-on participation in physics, electricity, life sciences, thermodynamics, weather, light, psychology, linguistics, and sense perception. The most popular exhibit is the soundproof, pitch-black Tactile Dome, through which visitors must find their way only by touch. Private groups often rent the dome to explore it in the nude. The Tactile Dome was designed by August Coppola, brother of filmmaker Francis Ford Coppola and father of actor Nicholas Cage. The pavilion in which the Exploratorium is located was originally used to house paintings and sculptures during the 1915 Panama-Pacific Exposition.

*Over 600,000 people per year explore the popular science museum.*

## FAIRMONT HOTEL

The Fairmont Hotel's gigantic lobby was re-created on a Hollywood sound stage for use in the television series *Hotel*. The Fairmont Hotel at California and Mason on Nob Hill was built on the property of James Fair. One of the Comstock lode silver kings, Fair had planned to construct a mansion on the site, but had built only the foundation when he died in 1894. Fair's daughter Tessie and her husband Hermann Oeirichs decided to build a hotel on the foundation instead, to the bewilderment of city officials, who could not understand why anyone would build a hotel so far from the center of town. It was almost ready to open when the 1906 fire gutted the interior. Work began all over again, and the hotel opened exactly one year to the day later. The penthouse at the Fairmont is the most expensive suite in the United States. The hotel has appeared in more than 50 movies, including *Vertigo* (1958) and *The Rock* (1996).

*The television series Hotel used the Fairmont for exterior scenes because it was producer Aaron Spelling's favorite hotel.*

## THE FARALLONES

The Ohlone tribe, all but wiped out by the Spanish in the early 19th century, believed their dead souls transmigrated to the Farallones, which they called the Islands of the Dead. These small granite islands 32 miles from the Pacific shore were first discovered by the Europeans during an expedition led by Juan Rodriguez Cabrillo in 1542 and incorporated into the city and county of San Francisco in 1872. Derived from the Spanish nautical expression for "small, rocky, pointed islands," the Farallones are inhospitable to humans, but are home to sea lions and some 250,000 birds. The Farallones were declared a bird sanctuary in 1907. A coast guard station and lighthouse, established in 1855, are on South Farallon atop Beacon Rock, 350 feet above sea level. Until 1968, a handful of families lived on South Farallon to operate the lighthouse. They had to climb a steep, winding path 320 feet up to the light, sometimes on their hands and knees during a gale or storm. Today an automated lighthouse and foghorns are used to warn ships.

*The Ohlone Indians, who inhabited the San Francisco Bay area for some 5,000 years, considered the islands sacred.*

## FERRY BUILDING

After the 1906 quake, the Ferry Building's clocks were stuck at 5:17 for a year. Opened in 1898 and modeled after the Cathedral Tower in Seville, Spain, the Ferry Building is located at the foot of Market Street. The clock tower is 230 feet high and for many years was the tallest building in San Francisco. Ferries left the building to points all over the bay, making it the second busiest passenger terminal in the world behind only London's Charring Cross Station. At the Ferry Building's peak, over 50 million passengers a year boarded 170 ferries. Its glory days as a hub for travelers and commuters ended with the building of the bridges. In 1956, the northern half of the structure was converted into office space, and six years later, the southern half was remodeled to house governmental agencies. Ferry service was discontinued in 1958, but was reinstated during the 1970s. A few ferries still operate to Oakland and Sausalito. The building serves as the headquarters of the San Francisco Port Authority. On the pier is a statue of Mahatma Gandhi, erected in 1988.

*The huge clocks on the Ferry Building tower stopped at the precise times of both the 1906 and the 1989 earthquakes.*

## 15 CENTS STREET

In addition to its nickname "15 Cents Street," Waverly Place, a two-block alley between Washington and Sacramento Streets just west of Grant Avenue in Chinatown, is also known as "the Street of Painted Balconies." Colorfully decorated facades and architectural details have been added to the three- and four-story Edwardian buildings erected just after the 1906 earthquake and fire. The colors are symbolic. Red stands for happiness, green for longevity, black for money, and yellow for good fortune. In addition to the three temples, the street is also home to many benevolent associations. From the street, pedestrians can hear the sound of drums booming from the upper floors, as association youth groups practice lion dance drills.

*At the turn of the century, 15 cents was the fee charged by the street's Chinese barbers for a haircut.*

## FILBERT STEPS

The steep Filbert Steps cling precariously to the sheer eastern slope of Telegraph Hill and lead down past the carefully maintained cottages of Darrell Place and Napier Lane beginning at the intersection of Filbert with Montgomery. The simple cottages date from the 1860s and 1870s. Napier Lane is the last remaining boardwalk in the city. Boardwalks were common in early San Francisco, but proved to be fire hazards and were replaced. The beautiful flowers and greenery that line the hillside are a labor of love for the residents of Filbert Steps. The landscaping was started in 1949 by 63-year-old ex-Hollywood movie actress and stunt woman Grace Marchant, who cleaned up the debris-strewn steps. She continued in her labor of love until she died in 1982. In 1878, a heavy rainstorm uncovered traces of gold near the Filbert Steps, dropped by returning prospectors decades earlier. A brief "gold rush" struck the area.

*A small bronze plaque on a bench on the Filbert Steps reads: "I have a feeling we're not in Kansas anymore."*

## FINANCIAL DISTRICT

Several pioneer businesses in the area used the address "Montgomery Street on the Beach" in their newspaper advertising. In the Gold Rush era, before landfill extended the waterfront, long wharves were built from Montgomery Street to deep anchorage in the bay. Commercial, Clay, and Washington Streets were built over the top of the old docks. The cross streets of Battery, Front, and Davis were originally planks that connected the wharves. The Financial District, roughly bounded by the Embarcadero and Mission, Third, Kearny, and Clay Streets, has been the city's core business district since banks started to appear in the 1850s to handle Gold Rush fortunes. When the Merchants Exchange Building was built at 465 California Street in 1903, it had a lookout tower on the roof to announce the arrival of ships. A flurry of high-rise office construction began in the mid-1960s, dramatically altering a skyline that had been essentially unchanged from 1930 until 1965. Ships abandoned during the Gold Rush have been unearthed during the construction of new buildings.

*Montgomery Street between Bush and Pacific was on the original shoreline of San Francisco Bay.*

## FIRE HYDRANT THAT SAVED NOE VALLEY

The fire hydrant at 20th and Church Streets in Noe Valley is painted gold because it saved the area from destruction in the 1906 earthquake and and fire. Noe Valley is a hilly, diverse neighborhood of quaint Victorian homes and businesses roughly bordered by 20th, Dolores, 30th, and Douglass Streets. It was part of the land grant of over 4,000 acres given to José de Jesus Noe in 1845 by California governor Pio Rico. Noe was San Francisco's last Mexican *alcalde* (mayor) in 1846 before the United States took control of the community during the Mexican War. Many streets in Noe Valley and the Mission District were named after early Mexican settlers like Noe, Castro, Guerrero, Alvarado, Sanchez, and Valencia. In 1854, John Horner, a wealthy produce merchant, purchased most of Noe's ranch and began selling lots to working-class Irish, Scandinavian, and German immigrants. Beginning in the 1970s, Noe Valley increasingly became the home of young professionals starting families.

*The lifesaving hydrant gets a fresh coat of paint every April 18, the anniversary of the 1906 earthquake.*

## FIRST PEDES-TRIAN ON THE GOLDEN GATE BRIDGE

May 27, 1937, was declared Pedestrian Day to inaugurate the Golden Gate Bridge. Local schools and most businesses closed for the day as people headed for the bridge's 6 A.M. opening. Donald Bryant, a San Francisco Junior College sprinter, was the first person across. Carmen Perez and her sister Minnie were the first to skate to the other side. Florentine Caligari was the first to make it on stilts. Two Balboa High School girls were the first twins to cross the bridge. There were people who walked backward, tap-danced, rode unicycles, and played musical instruments. Henry Boder, a 74-year-old San Franciscan who had crossed the Brooklyn Bridge on its opening day in 1883, repeated the feat on the Golden Gate. An estimated 200,000, each charged five cents, crossed the bridge on opening day. A day later, the Golden Gate Bridge opened for automobile traffic. Pedestrian Day was repeated on May 27, 1987, on the bridge's 50th anniversary as an estimated 800,000 people crossed the structure on foot. Their weight flattened the center span of the roadway, causing the bridge to drop 10 feet.

*Donald Bryant was the first person to cross the Golden Gate Bridge on foot.*

## FIRST TRANS-CONTINENTAL CALL

Alexander Graham Bell and his assistant Thomas Watson invented the telephone in Boston in 1876 by demonstrating that the human voice could be transmitted by wire. The pair were invited to participate in the first telephone conversation in history on January 25, 1915. Bell was in New York and Watson was at the office of the Pacific Telephone and Telegraph Company, at Grant and Bush Streets in San Francisco. Bell, then 67 years old, uttered his immortal words: "Mr. Watson, come here, I want you." San Francisco mayor James Rolph, New York mayor John Purroy Mitchel, and President Woodrow Wilson also took part in the historic occasion by placing long-distance calls.

*The first trans-continental telephone call was between New York City and San Francisco.*

## FISHERMAN'S WHARF

Today about 140 fishing boats dock at Fisherman's Wharf, only a third of which fish year-round. Up until the 1960s, Fisherman's Wharf was a flourishing fishing harbor and a significant part of the city's economy. The main harvest was salmon, crab, and prawns. The wharf was also home to railroad yards, warehouses, and large industrial plants. This center of the fishing industry was at the foot of Union and Filbert Streets for much of the late 19th century until it settled around the present location in about 1900, operated mainly by Italian immigrants. By the late 1950s, however, the fishing fleet was in decline due to overfishing and pollution, and much of Fisherman's Wharf was rundown or abandoned. A major renewal effort, including developments like Ghirardelli Square and the Cannery, revitalized the area. Pier 45, serving fish brokers, is one of the last working wharves on Fisherman's Wharf. The Buena Vista Cafe at 2765 Hyde Street is reputed to be the first location in America to serve Irish coffee. It was brought over by San Francisco newspaper columnist Stanton Delaplane, who discovered it one evening in an airport bar in Shannon, Ireland.

*At its peak in the 1940s, over 450 fishing boats docked at the wharf.*

## FOGHORNS

The coast guard ended an era in San Francisco in 1992 when it replaced the foghorns in San Francisco Bay with electronic signals that are less costly to operate and repair. Critics compared them to car alarms. Located at key spots around the bay, the foghorns each had a distinctive sound and were loved by most of the residents in the city. San Franciscans launched an immediate protest against their removal, and the coast guard allowed the nonprofit U.S. Lighthouse Society to reactivate the Alcatraz Island foghorns. The Golden Gate Bridge and Bay Bridge operate their own foghorns. The foghorns are triggered automatically when visibility is less than five miles at the mouth of the bay and less than two miles inside.

*Before foghorns were installed in 1903, ships were guided by cannons and bells.*

## FORT MASON

Former president Ronald Reagan was stationed briefly at Fort Mason during World War II, where he was in charge of loading convoys and attended war bond rallies. Located at the northwest corner of Van Ness Avenue and Bay Street adjoining Aquatic Park, Fort Mason occupies a section of waterfront on a bluff with spectacular views of the bay. The site was originally fortified with five cannons by the Spanish in 1797. It was taken over by squatters in the Gold Rush, then made into an army post during the Civil War. Some of the evicted squatter's homes were incorporated into the fort and used for officers' quarters. During World War II, it was embarkation point for 1.6 million troops and 23 tons of matériel en route to Pacific war zones. Soldiers during the Korean and Vietnam Wars also left for Asia from Fort Mason. In 1972 the fort's military duties were transferred to Oakland, and since 1977 the old warehouses have served as the headquarters for the Golden Gate National Recreation Area and have housed museums, theaters, classrooms, environmental organizations, and a restaurant.

*Ronald Reagan was stationed briefly at Fort Mason during World War II.*

## FORT POINT

Fort Point served as a construction base during the building of the Golden Gate Bridge. The only brick fort west of the Mississippi, Fort Point was built between 1853 and 1861 to guard San Francisco from sea attack. Fortified with 126 cannons with a range of two miles, it was obsolete shortly after it was finished. Its brick walls couldn't withstand the artillery developed during the Civil War, so it's fortunate that the fort was never attacked. Early explorers of the Bay Area observed a huge white cliff on the spot, but it was blasted away during construction of the fort. Fort Point was built atop the site of an abandoned Spanish gun battery erected in 1794. One of the cannons, cast in Spain in 1684, is located in the fort's museum. A Civil War–era cannon is fired twice daily for tourists. Jimmy Stewart rescued Kim Novak from drowning in the bay during a scene filmed at Fort Point in the 1958 movie *Vertigo*. Some of the sequence was filmed in a studio tank, however, because of the frigid bay currents.

*Fort Point was originally to be demolished to make way for the Golden Gate Bridge, but a redesign of the southern approach to the bridge left it intact.*

## FRISCO

The Outdoor Art League formed an Anti-Frisco Committee in 1907 to discourage the use of the term "Frisco." When present-day San Francisco was settled by the Mexicans, the tiny settlement was known as Yerba Buena, which has three meanings in the native Spanish language of the original settlers: "good grass," "good herb," and "peppermint." The mint grew wild in the area and was used to brew tea. The United States took control of the community from Mexico on July 9, 1846, when a band of 70 sailors and marines from the USS Portsmouth anchored in San Francisco Bay. John Montgomery was captain of the ship and, a month later, appointed 22-year-old Lieutenant Washington A. Bartlett as the first American *alcalde* (a combination mayor, judge, and sheriff). When leaders of a town on nearby Carquinez Strait (present-day Benicia) planned to name their new community Francisca, Bartlett headed them off by choosing San Francisco to replace the name Yerba Buena in a declaration issued on January 23, 1847. Bartlett wanted the town linked with the better-known San Francisco Bay. Bartlett served as San Francisco's mayor from 1883 through 1887.

*The nickname "Frisco" has long annoyed native San Franciscans.*

## FUGAZI HALL

Fugazi Hall was donated to the North Beach community by banker John Fugazi, the founder of what became the Transamerica Corporation. Located at 678 Green Street, it hosts *Beach Blanket Babylon,* the longest-running musical revue in theater history. Combining outlandish costumes, rock music, and topical humor, cabaret-style Beach Blanket Babylon has been playing to packed houses for over two decades. The show evolved from Steve Silver's Rent-a-Freak service, which consisted of a group who hired themselves out to entertain at parties dressed in zany costumes. *Beach Blanket Babylon* began at the Savoy-Tivoli, a North Beach bar, and proved so popular it moved into 400-seat Fugazi Hall in 1974. The show is best known for its oversize headdresses that resemble such local landmarks as the Golden Gate Bridge and the Transamerica Pyramid.

*Fugazi Hall was built in 1912 as a meeting hall for the North Beach neighborhood.*

## GHIRARDELLI SQUARE

Ghirardelli Square, bounded by Polk, Larkin, Beach, and North Point Streets, was bought by the sons of Domingo Ghirardelli in 1893 for the family's expanding chocolate business. The business was founded by the Italian-born Ghirardelli, who came to San Francisco in 1850. The Ghirardelli factory was located at 415 Jackson Street from 1857 until 1893 (in a building that is still standing). At its peak, the company employed 2,000 people. In the hall under the clock tower, which was added in 1916, are the German-made machines once used for making Ghirardelli Chocolate. The company moved its factory across San Francisco Bay to San Leandro in 1960, leaving the factory vacant. It was scheduled for demolition, but businessman William Roth proposed an innovative renovation, completed in 1967, blending old buildings with new shops and restaurants. Erected in 1915, Ghirardelli Square's red neon sign, a landmark visible for miles, was shut down during World War II for defense purposes.

*During the Civil War, part of the Ghirardelli Square complex was used by the Pioneer Woolen Mill, which produced uniforms for the Union Army.*

## GOLDEN GATE

The Golden Gate was named by John C. Frémont in 1848 in reference to the harbor in Constantinople called the Golden Horne. Three miles long and one mile wide, the passage links San Francisco Bay and the Pacific Ocean. For nearly two centuries, frequent fogs and a ragged irregular coastline conspired to conceal the entrance to San Francisco Bay from the mariners who sailed up and down the coast of California. Several stopped at the Farallon Islands, unaware of the break in the shoreline some 30 miles to the east. It was finally spotted by the party of Spanish explorer Don Gaspar de Portola on an inland expedition in 1769. When the United States acquired San Francisco in 1846, it was considered the greatest asset of the Far West. The Golden Gate caused numerous shipwrecks because of its currents, tidal surges, fog, and storms.

*An anti-submarine net was stretched across the Golden Gate during World War II.*

## GOLDEN GATE BRIDGE

Opened in 1937, the 4,200-foot suspension bridge was the longest in the world until 1959. The bridge is designed to sway 27 feet from east to west in a high wind or earthquake. It took four-and-a-half years and $35 million to build; in 1991, according to one estimate, it would cost $1.25 billion to reconstruct. The 746-foot towers of the Golden Gate Bridge were the world's tallest until 1997, when they were exceeded by a bridge in Denmark. The clearance between the roadbed and the water is 260 feet, a distance set by the military to allow ships to pass underneath. Over 2,000 lawsuits were filed in an attempt to prevent the bridge from being built. One of the first obstacles was winning the approval of the War Department. The military feared an enemy might bomb the bridge, which would block the harbor and the naval ships anchored there. The War Department granted permission for the bridge in exchange for control of the structure in time of war and for allowing government vehicles to cross free of charge.

*According to San Francisco psychiatrist Dr. Gerrit Blauvelt, San Franciscans' most common fear is gephydrophobia, the fear of crossing bridges.*

## GOLDEN GATE PARK

In the 1870s, western San Francisco, then referred to as the Outside Lands, was a refuge for outlaws. The beginnings of Golden Gate Park, bordered by Lincoln Way, the Great Highway, and Fulton and Stanyan Streets, were mired in difficulties. Squatters claimed the land, and it took years to remove them. Before development began in 1871, the area was just an arid, windswept tract of shifting sand dunes. Many experts believed that large trees could not be grown on the site, which had less water and more sand than any other section of the city. Newspapers derided the project as the "Great Sand Park." Nevertheless, the perseverance of William Hammond Hall, the original designer of the park, and John McLaren, supervisor from 1890 until 1943, transformed the barren sand into a 1,017-acre oasis. Among the features is the Children's Playground, opened in 1888 and the first playground constructed in an American park. It includes a restored carousel made in New York in 1912 and moved to the park in 1941. The Buffalo Paddock, hosting a small herd, has been a park feature since 1892.

*In the 1870s, workers in Golden Gate Park were advised to carry guns, as the park was then a haven for outlaws.*

## GRACE CATHEDRAL

Grace Cathedral, located in the block bounded by California, Taylor, Sacramento, and Jones Streets, was modeled after Notre Dame in Paris. It is one of the finest examples of Gothic architecture in the United States and is the third largest Episcopal cathedral in the country. It took 54 years to build and was finally consecrated in 1964. The Crocker family, which made a fortune in the railroad business, donated the land after their two mansions were lost in the 1906 earthquake and fire. The previous Grace Cathedral, built in 1860 at California and Stockton, was destroyed in the same disaster. The congregation was formed in 1849, when it met at Powell and Jackson. Martin Luther King, Jr. and Archbishop Desmond Tutu are among those who have preached at Grace Cathedral. The stained glass windows, installed in 1966, pay homage to such modern icons as Franklin Delano Roosevelt, Albert Einstein, Robert Frost, Thurgood Marshall, Henry Ford, Frank Lloyd Wright, and John Glenn.

*The danger of earthquakes led to the use of reinforced concrete and steel construction instead of the more conventional stone.*

## GRANT AVENUE

The section of Grant Avenue between Clay and Washington was originally laid in 1835 as the Calle de Fundación and formed the western boundary of the Old Plaza, now known as Portsmouth Square. When the street was first designated, the newly created Mexican village of Yerba Buena had fewer than 50 inhabitants. When the Americans took over in 1846, Calle de Fundación was renamed Dupont Street, after Samuel DuPont, one the captains of the USS *Portsmouth.* In 1876, the four blocks from Bush to Market were renamed Grant Avenue in honor of President Ulysses S. Grant, after Dupont Street had gained a rather unsavory reputation as a result of rampant vice. In 1906, the entire length of the roadway was named Grant Avenue. Many residents of Chinatown still refer to Grant Avenue as *Du Pon Gai,* which is Cantonese for Dupont Street.

*Grant Avenue was the first street in San Francisco.*

## HAAS-LILIENTHAL
## HOUSE

The 28-room Haas-Lilienthal House, built in the Queen Anne style between 1882 and 1886 at an original cost of $18,500, is located at 2007 Franklin between Jackson and Washington in Pacific Heights. Of the city's many gingerbread Victorians, this is one of the most flamboyant, with its bay windows, gables, turret, and abundant ornamentation. It was built for William Haas, a Bavarian immigrant who made a fortune as a wholesale grocer. His daughter, Alice Lilienthal, lived there until 1972, allowing the house to survive as the others in the neighborhood were demolished. The elaborate house is now a museum—its rooms fully furnished with period pieces from the late 1800s to the 1920s—and provides a glimpse of Victorian tastes and lifestyles. It also serves as the headquarters for the Foundation for San Francisco's Architectural Heritage.

*The Haas-Lilienthal House is the only fully furnished Victorian house in San Francisco open to the public.*

## HAIGHT-ASHBURY

In the late 19th century, Haight-Ashbury was a thriving middle-class neighborhood with over a thousand Victorian homes. When the neighborhood went into decline beginning in the 1920s, the big houses were divided into smaller and smaller apartments. In the late 1960s, the area was the mecca for hippies and became synonymous with youth rebellion and the counterculture. Janis Joplin lived in a one-room apartment with lover Country Joe McDonald at 112 Lyon Street in 1967. Graham Nash lived in the mansion at 737 Buena Vista West in the early 1970s. The house was built in 1887 by Richard Spreckels, nephew of the sugar magnate. Previous residents included Jack London and Ambrose Bierce. The house at 710 Ashbury Street was the Grateful Dead commune from 1966 through 1968. The back of Jefferson Airplane's *Surrealistic Pillow* album features 130 Delmar Street. "Flower Power" faded quickly, and by the early 1970s, the Haight deteriorated into a skid row. During the 1980s, however, it enjoyed a gentrified revival.

*The word hippie was a derisive term coined by the Beats, who called their 1960s counter-cultural counterparts "junior hipsters."*

## HALLADIE BUILDING

The revolutionary glass curtain at the front of the Halladie Building, which hangs a foot in front of the reinforced concrete frame of the structure, is now a common feature of modern office buildings. The Halladie Building at 130 Sutter Street was built as an investment by the University of California and named after Andrew Halladie, developer of the cable car, who was a regent at the school. Originally, the wrought-iron fire escapes were painted in the school colors of blue and gold. Born in London of Scottish parentage in 1836, Halladie arrived in California in 1852. His father was one of the inventors of wire rope, and Halladie drew on his father's expertise to construct a haulage system used to pull cars up a track in the gold mines of the Sierra Nevada. At the age of 19, Halladie designed and built a 220-foot wire suspension bridge and aqueduct across the middle fork of the American River. His father also owned a patent on a wire cable grip that was used to grasp ore buckets on an overhead cable. Utilizing this expertise, Halladie sank his entire fortune on developing the world's first cable car line in San Francisco in 1873.

*Built in 1917, the Halladie Building was the first in the world to use glass-curtain wall construction.*

## HERB CAEN WAY

*San Francisco Chronicle* columnist Herb Caen coined the term *beatnik* in 1957, combining the Beat Generation with the recently launched Russian satellite *Sputnik*. Born in Sacramento in 1916, Herb Caen came to San Francisco in 1936 and landed a job with the *Chronicle*. Two years later, he began a column at the newspaper that continued until his death from lung cancer in 1997. His upbeat columns combined news, gossip, satire, anecdotes, and love of San Francisco, which he pounded out with two fingers on a Royal typewriter. The vignettes were punctuated with three dots. The power of his columns was so strong that few dared to cross him. Known as "Mr. San Francisco," he won a special Pulitzer Prize for his "continuing contribution as a voice and conscience of his city."

A 3.2-mile stretch of the Embarcadero was renamed Herb Caen Way in 1997.

## HIGHEST POINT
## IN SAN FRANCISCO

Mount Davidson, the city's highest point, was named in 1911 for George Davidson, who surveyed it in 1862 for the U.S. Coast and Geodetic Survey. Previously, it had been known as Blue Mountain. Located between Portola Drive, O'Shaugnessy Boulevard, and Monterey Boulevard, it dwarfs such better-known neighbors as Nob Hill (376 feet above sea level), Russian Hill (294 feet), Telegraph Hill (284 feet), and Pacific Heights (370 feet). Easter sunrise services have been held at the base of the 103-foot-high cross atop the promontory since 1923. The present cross dates from 1934 and is the fifth on the site. It was originally designed to be 100 feet tall, but there was enough extra concrete left over to add three feet. The cross was lit every evening until 1989, when a group challenged the constitutionality of a religious display on city-owned land. Easter services are still held on Mount Davidson, but the cross remains unlit. The lowest point in San Francisco, the corner of Fifth and Berry, is 5.71 feet below sea level.

*At 938 feet above sea level, Mount Davidson is the highest point in San Francisco.*

## HOTEL THAT CLEANS COINS

The practice of cleaning coins began after the St. Francis Hotel received complaints from women that the coins soiled their white gloves. Although white gloves have long passed out of fashion, the hotel still washes its change today. Now the Westin St. Francis, located on the Powell Street side of Union Square, the hotel cleans 20,000 to 25,000 coins each day. A custom-built set of machines soaks, cleans, polishes, rinses, and sorts the coins. The "coin laundry" uses lead shot and Boraxo soap. As the machine rotates, the coins are rinsed, separated from the shot, dried under 250 watt bulbs, counted, and repackaged. Arnold Batliner was the coin washer from 1962 until he retired in 1993 at the age of 88. The clean coins are known around town as "St. Francis money."

*The St. Francis Hotel began washing and polishing its coins daily in 1939.*

## HYDE STREET
## CABLE CAR

Gloria Sykes was a 23-year-old who in 1964 had recently moved to San Francisco from Michigan when she was thrown against a pole inside a careening Hyde Street cable car. She suffered only bruises, but sued the city for psychic injuries. According to her attorney, the accident unleashed emotions hidden "deep in the closet of her mind." Sykes said that the accident left her with an intense need for "the vibrations of the male body." She claimed the incident caused her to have an insatiable desire for sex that could be prompted by a mere meeting of eyes on the streets, resulting in hundreds of sexual liaisons, including as many as 50 in a five-day period. The suit, dubbed the "Cable Car Named Desire," was heard before a jury of four men and eight women, which deliberated eight hours before awarding Sykes $50,000.

*A woman sued the city for $500,000, claiming that a cable car accident turned her into a nymphomaniac.*

## HYDE STREET PIER

Several restored historic vessels are docked at the Hyde Street Pier at the foot of Hyde Street, which is part of the Maritime National Historical Park System. The three open to the public are the sidewheel ferry *Eureka* (built in 1890), the three-masted wooden sailing schooner *C. A. Thayer* (1895), and the three-masted square-rigger *Balclutha* (1883). The *Balclutha,* built in Scotland, was used in the 1935 film *Mutiny on the Bounty.* During its days as a cargo ship, it made 17 trips around Cape Horn. The *Eureka* was once the largest passenger ferry in the world, capable of carrying 2,300 passengers and 120 cars. It is loaded with vintage cars and trucks. The *C. A. Thayer* was once used by the army as a barge to store empty shells from target practice at sea. The scow-schooner *Alma* (1891) and the paddle-wheel steam tug *Eppleton Hall* (1914) are also located at the pier. The ships hold artifacts, photography collections, and displays from their sailing days. Originally, Hyde Street Pier was used for ferries before the bridges were built.

Comedian Jonathan Winters was briefly institutionalized in 1959 after he climbed the masting of the Balclutha and shouted, "I am the man in the moon."

## I LEFT MY HEART
## IN SAN FRANCISCO

"I Left My Heart in San Francisco,"
composed by Douglass Cross and
George Cory in 1954, became famous with
Tony Bennett's 1962 recording. It was made the
official song of the city of San Francisco in a ceremony
held on October 6, 1969. Still, many preferred "San Francisco,"
sung by Jeanette MacDonald to Clark Cable in the 1936 movie *San
Francisco*. In the film, MacDonald was belting out the song
in a barroom as the 1906 earthquake hit the city. "San
Francisco," with its lyrics by Gus Kahn and melody by
Bronislaw Kaper and Walter Jerman, also became the
official song of San Francisco on May 15, 1984. "Everybody thinks we're a kooky city anyway," said Board of
Supervisors member Willie Kennedy. "Why not have two
official songs?"

*Tony Bennett
first sang "I Left
My Heart in
San Francisco"
at the Fairmont
Hotel's Venetian
Room.*

## INTERNATIONAL ORANGE

The red-orange color of the Golden Gate Bridge is somewhat of an accident. When the towers were constructed, they were coated in the red-orange primer, which was extended to the rest of the bridge as work continued. Designers of the bridge liked the way the distinctive color complemented the hills of Marin County and provided a contrast to the fog that swirled through the towers, so the bridge remained International Orange. It also increases the visibility of the bridge in fog. The top coat of orange is replaced constantly because the auto exhaust and chilly, salty air eats away at the finish. A team is employed full-time to apply about two tons of the coloring per week to keep the paintwork in good condition and prevent the bridge from rusting. It takes four years to apply one coat. The job is not for the faint-hearted. Painters have to be able to climb to the top of the bridge's 746-foot towers and routinely brave 30-mile-per-hour winds.

*The official name for the color of the Golden Gate Bridge is International Orange.*

## JACK KEROUAC
## STREET

Jack Kerouac and the Beat Generation emerged during the 1950s and
moved into North Beach. Like many, the
Beats were frustrated by the conservative political climate of the time and challenged most of the social
conventions of the era. They gathered for poetry readings and
jazz concerts, dressed in black, and dropped out of the main-
stream. Whatever impact the Beats might have had was
trivialized by their caricaturing in the media and by the
tourists that poured into North Beach for "Beatnik Tours."
Vesuvio's, across Jack Kerouac Street from City Lights
Bookstore at 255 Columbus Avenue, was a favorite hang-
out of the Beats. Kerouac and Dylan Thomas were among
those who drank at the bar, which was opened in 1949 by
Frenchman Henri Lenoir Vesuvio. The bar serves no food
but welcomes patrons to bring their lunch and have a
drink. The walls are crammed with photos and memora-
bilia from the beatnik era. The Tosca Cafe, at 242
Columbus, was another hallowed beatnik gathering spot.

*Jack Kerouac,
author of* On
the Road, *was
one of the first
Beat Genera-
tion writers
who came to
San Francisco
from New York.*

## JACKSON SQUARE

A vicious gang of criminals from Australia, who frequented Jackson Square in the Barbary Coast days, would shout "huddle 'em" when they assaulted their victims. The phrase sounded like *hoodlum* when spoken with an Australian accent. Jackson Square, bordered by Columbus Avenue and Pacific, Washington, and Sansome Streets, contains the only group of downtown business buildings to escape the 1906 earthquake and fire. The area was saved by Navy Lieutenant Frederick Newton, who ran a mile-long hose from Pier 43 over Telegraph Hill. Located in the area is what survives of San Francisco's Gold Rush era. Most of the structures date to the 1850s, when the shoreline and docks were just east of Montgomery Street. The block of Jackson Street between Montgomery and Kearny was the site of the old Laguna Salada, a small inlet crossed by a footbridge built in 1844, the first bridge constructed in San Francisco. In disrepair by the 1950s, designers and furniture dealers moved into the neighborhood and preserved its historic buildings as showplaces.

*The word hoodlum had its derivation in Jackson Square in the 1850s when the area was known as the Barbary Coast.*

# JAPANESE
# TEA GARDEN

The tea garden, featuring a pagoda, gates, statuary, and a tea house, was built for the 1894 Midwinter International Exhibition by San Franciscan George Turner Marsh, who was born in Australia and spent his teenage years in Japan. After the fair, Hagiwara, a Japanese gardener, took care of the garden. He offered fortune cookies, hard pieces of pastry holding fortune-telling messages printed on paper, as a novelty to visitors. The cookies proved to be such a hit that Chinese restaurants in San Francisco's Chinatown adopted the idea and served them as a Chinese tradition, even though the cookies didn't exist in China. Unfortunately, Hagiwara never bothered to patent his invention. By the time of his death in 1925, Hagiwara had expanded the garden from its original one acre to five. The Hagiwara family cared for the garden until 1942 when they were placed in an internment camp in the wake of anti-Japanese hysteria following the bombing of Pearl Harbor. Until 1952, the Japanese Tea Garden was called the Oriental Tea Garden. A bronze statue was erected in honor of the Hagiwara family in 1974.

*Makoto Hagiwara, creator of the Japanese Tea Garden in Golden Gate Park, invented the fortune cookie in 1909.*

## JAPANTOWN

Japantown once covered about 40 blocks of the Western Addition, but the thousands of residents of Japanese ancestry, including American citizens, who had settled in the area were forced to move in 1942 after war was declared on Japan. Most were placed in internment camps in remote areas of California, Utah, and Idaho. Many left the camps to join the American Armed Forces in segregated all-Japanese units. The Japanese 442nd Regimental Combat Team was the most decorated American military unit of the war. After the war, the Japanese population dispersed throughout the Bay Area. Today, only about 4 percent of San Francisco's Japanese-American population lives in Japantown. In a spirit of reconciliation, San Francisco opened the Japan Center in 1968, a shopping, dining, and entertainment complex bounded by Post, Sutter, Laguna, and Fillmore Streets, a generation after World War II. The Peace Pagoda in the complex, a gift from the Japanese people designed by Yoshiro Taniguchi, rises 110 feet above the plaza in five copper-roofed concrete tiers.

*Japantown is also known as Nihonmachi, which means "Japanese Town" in Japanese.*

## KEZAR STADIUM

Located in the southeast corner of Golden Gate Park, and built in 1925 with room for 59,000 fans, Kezar Stadium was the home of the San Francisco 49ers from their debut in 1946 until they moved to Candlestick Park in 1971. The 49ers were originally part of the All-American Football Conference and moved to the National Football League in 1950 after the AAFC merged with the NFL. When the Oakland Raiders were formed in 1960 as an original member of the American Football League, the team lacked an adequate place to play in the East Bay. The Raiders played at Kezar Stadium in 1960 and at Candlestick Park in 1961 before moving to Frank Youell Field in Oakland in 1962. The team began play at Oakland-Alameda County Stadium in 1966. Reduced to a capacity of 10,000, Kezar Stadium is currently used for high school sports.

*Kezar Stadium was the site of the first games of both the San Francisco 49ers and the Oakland Raiders.*

## KONG CHOW TEMPLE

A reading at the Kong Chow Temple for President Truman's wife in 1948 predicted her husband would win the presidential election in November. At the time, Truman's election chances against Thomas Dewey looked hopeless, but the fortune came true. The Kong Chow Temple, which opened on Pine Street in 1857, is considered to be the oldest Chinese temple in the United States. It was founded by immigrants from Kong Chow province and is one of the Chinese Six Companies, an influential Chinatown association. Kong Chow Temple has been at 855 Stockton Street on the fourth floor above the post office since 1977. Typical of many Chinatown temples, it is located on the top floor of the building. Many of the original furnishings survive. The altar and statuary are also possibly the oldest Chinese religious shrines in North America. One altar is known to have been carved in Canton, China, in the 19th century and shipped to San Francisco. The artifacts were rescued from the 1906 fire before the original temple was destroyed by dynamite in an attempt to check the flames.

*President Harry Truman's wife Margaret had her fortune told at the Kong Chow Temple in June 1948.*

## LAFAYETTE PARK

Lafayette Park, bordered by Gough, Sacramento, Laguna, and Washington Streets, was reserved as a public park in 1855.

It was mostly a barren sand hill and a haven for squatters, however, until the 1910s. One of those squatters was Sam Holladay, a former city attorney and stage driver who built a large white house in 1867, called Holladay's Heights, at the park's summit. He also constructed an astronomical observatory on the hill in 1879, the first in the West. The tenacious Holladay even instructed city gardeners as if the land were his own and defied all attempts to evict him, including legal action that went all the way to the Supreme Court. The intrusive Holladay house was finally torn down in 1936. The trees he planted around the house still grow at the peak of the park, which is 378 feet above sea level, the highest point in Pacific Heights.

*A private mansion stood in the middle of the public park from 1867 until 1936.*

## LAST RIVET

Sonoma, California, resident Charles Segerstrom had the bright idea that the "last" rivet placed in the Golden Gate Bridge should be made of gold. The rivet, valued at $400, was fashioned from gold mined from the historic old Southern mines district of Gold Rush fame. On April 27, 1937, after numerous speeches and much pomp and ceremony, the rivet was handed to Edward Stanley, the man who drove the first rivet in the bridge. Stanley's pneumatic hammer was made to use on steel, not on soft gold, and fine particles of gold were showered in the face of spectators. The head of the rivet fell off and disappeared into the water. The remainder of the rivet was punched out, and it too plunged into the depths of the bay. The bridge was unceremoniously finished off with a steel rivet.

*Charles Segerstrom donated the symbolic "last" rivet installed in the Golden Gate Bridge.*

## LEVI'S PLAZA

Award-winning Levi's Plaza, the corporate headquarters of Levi Strauss and Co., was completed in 1982 on Filbert Street between Sansome and Battery at the foot of Telegraph Hill. The setbacks of the buildings were designed to harmonize with the varying architectural styles of the surrounding area. Because of the collegiate atmosphere of the complex, it is also known as Levi Strauss University. The fountain is built of granite from the Sierra Nevada, where miners first wore the world-famous jeans. The brig *Palmyra*, abandoned during the Gold Rush, lies underneath the fountain. An 1879 ice house and a 1903 warehouse were incorporated into the complex. The gate across Union Street next to the ice house was built by a movie company for a scene in the 1971 film *The Organization*, starring Sidney Poitier. The jeans are manufactured at 250 Valencia Street in the Mission District in a factory built in 1906.

*A display of some of the company's failed products includes colorful women's jeans that were advertised in tandem with Jell-O products.*

## LINCOLN PARK

Lincoln Park at 34th and Clement Streets is a 270 acre open space along the headlands of Point Lobos. The surf crashing against 200-foot cliffs adds to the drama of the breathtaking view of the Golden Gate Bridge and the bay. The California Palace of the Legion of Honor and the Lincoln Park Municipal Golf Course are located in the park. Lincoln Park was originally used as a cemetery, mostly for paupers and Chinese immigrants, beginning in 1870. The practice was continued until 1901 when San Francisco prohibited burials within city limits. The city purchased the cemetery for Lincoln Park in 1909, and the many of the graves were left undisturbed. Thousands of San Francisco's former citizens still lie under the park, a few of which were accidentally unearthed during the renovation of the California Palace of the Legion of Honor during the 1990s. Near the first tee of the golf course is an arch from a Chinese tomb.

*Located in Lincoln Park is part of the battle-torn bridge of the USS San Francisco, which was damaged in the World War II Battle of Guadalcanal.*

## LOTTA'S FOUNTAIN

In 1990, an aftershock registering 5.4 on the Richter scale jolted the annual gathering of survivors of the 1906 earthquake held at Lotta's Fountain. The fountain, at the busy intersection of Geary, Kearny, and Market, was a gift to the city from entertainer Lotta Crabtree, who was a 19th-century combination of Shirley Temple and Madonna. She wowed Gold Rush audiences as a child stage star and as an adult appeared in New York on Broadway. She died in 1924 with a $4 million fortune. Erected in 1875, the fountain has been altered since its installation. Originally, tin cups were chained to the base for communal use and water troughs were installed for horses. There was a commotion at the dedication of the fountain because of a rumor that the fountain spewed beer. A small riot ensued when many in the crowd were angered that it dispensed only water. In 1916, the base of the fountain was raised and eight feet were added to the shaft to bring the fountain more in line with the street lamps on Market Street. It has also been moved a few feet to the southeast.

*It is a tradition for San Franciscans to meet at Lotta's Fountain every April 18 at 5:12 A.M. to commemorate the anniversary of the 1906 earthquake and fire.*

## LUCKY HOUSES

Octagonal houses, popularized by the book *A Home for All,* were purported as lucky and healthful for their occupants because they let in more air and light. Some 700 were built nationwide, five of which were in San Francisco. Of the city's two surviving eight-sided houses, the Octagon House, located at the corner of Union and Gough in Pacific Heights, was originally built in a lot across the street in 1861. It was indeed a lucky house as only one of the eight walls collapsed in the 1906 earthquake. The house was moved to its present location in 1952 after its purchase, for one dollar, by the California chapter of the National Society of Colonial Dames for use as the organization's headquarters. The Octagon House also serves as a museum of antiques and decorative arts from the Colonial and Federal periods. The other octagonal house is a private residence on Green Street, built in 1857, and has been extensively remodeled. It was even luckier during the 1906 earthquake and fire. The house was one of the few on Russian Hill to escape total destruction from the flames.

*Octagonal houses were an architectural fad after the publication of Orson Squire Fowler's book A Home for All.*

## M. H. DE YOUNG
## MEMORIAL MUSEUM

The 1894 California Midwinter International Exposition, for which the M. H. de Young Memorial Museum was built, was spearheaded by Michael de Young, co-founder of the *San Francisco Chronicle*, as a way to promote the city and its winter climate. It was located on 180 acres at the eastern end of Golden Gate Park. Pavilions from 37 countries were represented, attracting 2.5 million visitors. The highlight of the fair was the 266-foot Electric Tower, erected at a time when electricity was still a novelty. The beam from the tower was so powerful that one could read a newspaper by its light six miles away. After the fair closed, organizers refused to pay for the tower's removal, so park commissioner John McLaren had it blown up in 1897. During the fair, the present-day museum building housed the fine arts section, and de Young persuaded the city to preserve it and initiated the building program to expand the museum's size and collections. The galleries, which surround a central courtyard, feature American paintings, sculpture, and decorative arts from the Americas and Africa and a selection of British art from the 16th through 19th centuries.

*The M. H. de Young Memorial Museum is the only building remaining from the 1894 California Midwinter International Exposition.*

## MAIDEN LANE

Maiden Lane, which runs from Stockton to Kearny Streets just east of Union Square, was known as Morton Street during the Barbary Coast era. It was a violent, hellish red-light district until the 1906 fire devoured the bordellos. Topless prostitutes sat at open windows and solicited passersby. Some of the call girls claimed to entertain as many as 100 customers a day. The street emerged as a shopping district after the city was rebuilt following the earthquake and fire, and the name was changed to Maiden Lane during the 1920s to erase its infamous reputation. It is now lined with elegant and pricey designer shops and art galleries. The building located at 140 Maiden Lane is the only one in San Francisco designed by Frank Lloyd Wright. Designed in 1948, it features a spiral ramp and skylights, a smaller version of the one Wright built for the Guggenheim Museum in New York City, which opened in 1959. Wright's scheme was originally a complete transformation of a 1911 warehouse for the V. C. Morris store, which sold china and crystal, linen, and other fine housewares. The brick facade has an arched entryway.

*Known as Morton Street until 1906, Maiden Lane was the scene of some 100 murders a year during the late 19th century.*

## MARINA DISTRICT

In 1915 the Marina District was created from landfill as the site for the Panama-Pacific International Exposition. During construction of the fair, 635 acres of marshland were filled in and a seawall was built along the shoreline. Once the exposition was over, the temporary buildings were removed and real estate speculators took over. Through the 1920s, developers laid out streets on the former fairgrounds and built the pastel, stucco Mediterranean revival houses, apartments, and shops that now make up the Marina District along the bay between Fort Mason, the Presidio, and Pacific Heights. The dredging of the bay produced enough deep water to build a yacht harbor. The unstable landfill gave way during the 1989 earthquake, causing the collapse of numerous buildings. Ironically, some of the landfill on which the Marina District was created consisted of debris dumped from the 1906 earthquake.

*Before 1915, the Marina District didn't exist at all.*

## MARKET STREET

When 120-foot wide Market Street was first surveyed in 1847, a 60-foot sand dune stood at the present-day intersection with Second Street. Another dune 190 feet in height was a few hundred yards west. Market Street cuts diagonally at a 36-degree angle across the gridiron street pattern of San Francisco from the Ferry Building to Twin Peaks. It forms a boundary between the northern and southern parts of the city, dividing the prestigious area north of Market (sometimes called Above Market) and the industrial and working-class section south of the street (popularly known as SOMA). The creation of Market Street was part of the street plan proposed in 1847 by Irish-born surveyor Jasper O'Farrell. It was by far the most controversial aspect of his plan because few of the streets on either side of Market intersected and the blocks south of Market were four times larger than those north of the boulevard. The plan, though adopted, met with stiff opposition, and O'Farrell went into hiding for several weeks until tempers cooled. South of Market is also known as "South of the Slot" because of the cable car line that ran down the center of the boulevard.

*In 1847, when Market Street was first surveyed, it featured huge sand dunes.*

### MARK HOPKINS HOTEL

The mansion which stood on the current site of the Mark Hopkins Hotel was built in 1878 and consumed in the fire of 1906. Scars from the fire are still visible on the wall that surrounded the extravagant mansion built by railroad magnate Mark Hopkins and his wife on Nob Hill at California and Mason Streets. George D. Smith, builder of the hotel, tried to remove the wall by blasting, but it proved to be impregnable. The hotel opened in 1925. The 19th floor was the private apartment of copper magnate D. C. Jackling until 1939 when it was remodeled as the Top of the Mark, the forerunner of all restaurant–view lounges. Thousands of World War II servicemen drank a last toast at the bar, often with their wives or girlfriends, before leaving for overseas. The women frequently returned to watch their loved one's ship sail out of the bay, causing the western corner to be called "weeper's corner."

*The granite wall around the Mark Hopkins Hotel originally surrounded the Mark Hopkins mansion.*

## MCLAREN LODGE

Built in 1896, McLaren Lodge now serves as the headquarters of San Francisco's Recreation and Parks Department. It was Scottish-born John McLaren who shaped Golden Gate Park at a time when many regarded it as a wasteland. Affectionately called "Uncle John," he accomplished a horticultural miracle by relentlessly planting and growing grass, plants, shrubs, and trees where before there was nothing but arid, windswept sand dunes and brush. McLaren battled regularly with City Hall, thwarting the efforts of politicians to tamper with his vision, once blocking a cable car line from entering the park. A special law was passed in 1917 exempting the park superintendent from the city's mandatory retirement age of 70. McLaren became almost an absolute ruler over his "kingdom." He hated statuary and planted shrubbery in front of them. One of the edicts of this gifted and single-minded landscape genius was no "Keep Off The Grass" signs.

*Mission-style McLaren Lodge, at Fell and Stanyan Streets, was the home of John McLaren, superintendent of Golden Gate Park from 1890 until his death in 1943.*

# MIGHTY CASEY AND THE MUDVILLE NINE

Ernest Thayer was a humor columnist for the *San Francisco Examiner*, which was published by his Harvard classmate William Randolph Hearst, and wrote under the byline "Phin." Thayer's 112-line poem *Casey at the Bat* appeared in the paper on June 3, 1888. The verse told the terrible tale of the Mudville Nine and the Mighty Casey, who struck out. Thayer was a regular contributor to the newspaper, but by the time it was published, he had returned to his hometown of Worcester, Massachusetts, to run a family-owned textile mill. *Casey at the Bat* was clipped by an unknown reader, who sent it to actor DeWitt Hopper. Hopper recited the poem at Wallach's Theater in New York City before an audience that included members of the New York Giants and the Chicago Cubs. The verse quickly launched debate as to who wrote it and whether it was based on actual events. Lacking a copyright claim, Thayer never received a penny for his creation.

San Francisco Examiner *humor columnist Ernest Thayer penned the famous poem* Casey at the Bat.

## MISSION DISTRICT

Until the building of a long plank road which connected the Mission District with downtown, the insect-plagued, swampy terrain of what is now South of Market made the area inaccessible. The Mission District, the neighborhood that surrounds Mission Dolores, was Hispanic in character at its outset and is Hispanic in character today. In between, the area has seen a parade of nationalities. Scandinavian and German settlers moved in beginning in the 1860s, followed by the Irish and Italians. The international flavor of the area resulted in a Brooklynesque accent known as the Mish. In the late 1800s, the district was filled with gambling houses, dance halls, amusement parks, and racetracks. Balmy Alley and Lucky Alley were named after famous racehorses of the day. Woodward Gardens, a popular 19th-century botanical garden with a playground and zoo, was located at 13th and Mission. A few wealthy families built lavish weekend homes in the area. In the 1960s, when immigrants from Mexico and South and Central America settled in the area, the neighborhood's Latino atmosphere was reasserted.

*In 1851, the Mission District was linked with downtown by a 40-foot-wide wooden-plank road along Mission Street from Third to 16th Streets.*

## MISSION DOLORES

Spanish settlers led by Captain José Moraga and Father Francisco Palou founded San Francisco's first mission in 1776, originally built near the corner of Camp and Albion Streets, two blocks east of the present location of Mission Dolores. Formally called the Mission San Francisco de Assisi, this was the sixth of 21 missions built between 1769 and 1823 by the Franciscans along El Camino Real, which linked the missions from Mexico to Sonoma, California. Constructed by Costanoan Indians, the present mission building was completed in 1791 and is the oldest structure still standing in San Francisco. Its four-foot-thick adobe walls have helped the building survive four major earthquakes. After Spain secularized the missions in 1834, Mission Dolores was used for a hotel, a dance hall, then a brewery, until it was reacquired by the Catholic church in 1857. The wooden trusses, originally strapped together with rawhide, were reinforced with steel beams in 1918. The Basilica of San Francisco is next door to the mission.

In 1776, a lake called Laguna de Nuestra Señora de los Dolores (Lake of Our Lady of Sorrows) covered the area now bounded by 15th, Guerrero, 23rd, and Harrison Streets.

## MISSION DOLORES CEMETERY

Kim Novak's character came to the Mission Dolores cemetery in the Alfred Hitchcock film *Vertigo* to visit the fictitious grave of her great-grandmother Carlotta Valdes, whose identity she assumed. The tombstone of Valdes remained for several years and became a tourist attraction, but was eventually removed by church officials. Among those interred in the cemetery are Father Palou, one of the founders of Mission Dolores; Francisco de Haro, the first *alcalde*, or mayor, of Yerba Buena; and Luis Antonio Arguello, the first governor of California under Mexican rule. In addition to historical figures, more than 5,500 native Costanoan Indians are buried in unmarked graves in the cemetery garden, most having died during early 19th-century measles epidemics transmitted by white settlers. A statue of Junípero Serra looms over the graves of Spanish, Mexican, and American pioneers as well as three victims of the 1850s vigilantes. Burials took place at Mission Dolores from the 1780s until the city banned them in 1901.

*The cemetery was a key location in the 1958 Alfred Hitchcock film Vertigo.*

## MONTGOMERY STREET

A copper plaque on the corner of Montgomery and Merchant Streets marks the site of the end of the Pony Express's 1,966-mile journey from St. Joseph, Missouri, which took 10 to 13 days. Persistent rains and the crush of new arrivals during the winter of 1849–50 turned the dirt street, then on the shoreline, into a sea of mud. Several animals and at least four people sank into the ooze and drowned. The building at 730 Montgomery, dating from about 1852, housed the *Golden Era,* a popular weekly established in 1854 that published works by Mark Twain and Bret Harte. The Montgomery Block, a four-story office building nicknamed the "Monkey Block," occupied the present site of the Transamerica Pyramid between 1853 and 1959. A proposal to widen Montgomery after the 1906 earthquake was thwarted by a single property owner who refused to relinquish the necessary frontage.

*The Pony Express, carrying mail from the East, stopped at Montgomery and Merchant Streets in 1860–61.*

## MOSCONE CONVENTION CENTER

After decades-long conflicts among residents, city planners, and developers, the Moscone Convention Center was completed in 1981. Later additions were made in 1988 and 1991. Occupying the block bounded by Howard, Folsom, Third, and Fourth Streets, the modern center encloses 300,000 square feet of exhibition space. Its signature is the contemporary glass-and-girder lobby at street level and a column-free interior. The convention center is named after George Moscone, the only San Francisco mayor assassinated while in office. Both Moscone and Harvey Milk, a member of the San Francisco Board of Supervisors and the first openly gay individual to hold elective office in the United States, were killed in their City Hall offices by Dan White, a former supervisor and city policeman and fireman. The convention center's lobby once displayed a ceramic bust of Moscone by sculptor Robert Arneson, but graphic images on the supporting column were deemed controversial and the work was removed.

*The 1984 Democratic Party convention, nominating Walter Mondale and Geraldine Ferraro, was held at Moscone Center.*

## NAMES PROJECT

The NAMES Project at 2362 Market Street in the Castro District is a volunteer, nonprofit organization for those who create the panels of remembrance that form the AIDS quilt. Sections of the quilt have been exhibited around the world to commemorate those who have died of AIDS and to draw attention to the disease. It has been on The Mall in Washington, D C., and at the White House several times. The project was started in 1987 by gay rights activist Cleve Jones. The quilt panels each measure three feet by six feet, the size of a gravesite, and are sewn together in groups of eight. There are panels for Arthur Ashe, Rock Hudson, and Freddie Mercury. Each quilt reflects the personality and interests of the individual who succumbed to AIDS.

*If the AIDS quilt were displayed in its entirety, it would cover 14 football fields.*

## NATIONAL MARITIME MUSEUM

The National Maritime Museum in Aquatic Park dates from 1939 and served a variety of purposes before being converted to its present use in 1951. The building, in the streamline moderne style, resembles a luxury liner, with porthole windows, ship's-wheel door handles and three tiers evoking decks. Originally the Aquatic Park Casino, the structure was designed not for gambling, as the name might suggest, but to provide changing rooms, restaurants, and banquet halls for the intended 5,000 bathers expected to visit the park each day. But the water was too cold and few came, so the casino became an expensive flop. The museum contains ship models, books, photographs, maps, and instruments chronicling San Francisco nautical history.

*When the building housing the museum first opened, it was intended as a lavish boathouse.*

## NEIMAN-MARCUS

The Neiman-Marcus building incorporates the rotunda from the old City of Paris department store, which was located at the southeast corner of Geary and Stockton Streets facing Union Square from 1896 until 1981. The original Renaissance-style, baroque-ornamented building was destroyed in the 1906 earthquake and fire and reopened in 1909 with a soaring four-story, amber-colored, stained-glass rotunda as its centerpiece. The dome, framed by enameled, wrought-iron balconies, depicted a sailing ship and the emblem of Paris, France. The City of Paris was named after the ship that carried store founder Felix Verdier to America from Europe in 1850. When the store closed in 1981, many San Franciscans vigorously protested the destruction of the historic building. When Neiman-Marcus built on the site, the dome was incorporated into the entrance of the new store. A huge Christmas tree is decorated under the dome during the holiday season.

*The Neiman-Marcus rotunda was part of the old City of Paris department store.*

## NEPTUNE SOCIETY COLUMBARIUM

The four-story Neptune Society Columbarium at 1 Lorraine Court in the Richmond District holds the ashes of thousands of San Franciscans, including many prominent pioneer families. About 10,000 of the 30,000 niches remain vacant. The niches are decorated by the families of the deceased with items such as dolls from the television series *The Munsters* and golf clubs. The Columbarium was built in 1898 as part of the Odd Fellows Cemetery, which opened in 1865 on 37 acres and closed in 1937 when most of the graves were exhumed and moved to Colma in San Mateo County. Houses were constructed over the old cemetery, and prospective homeowners were warned that due to a lack of funds, some of the graves were not removed. The building is also known for its domed ceiling, stained-glass windows, and acoustics. Two people standing on opposite sides can carry on a conversation spoken in whispers.

*Set in a two-acre garden, the Neptune Society Columbarium is the only cemetery for cremated remains in San Francisco.*

## NEW
## MONTGOMERY STREET

During the 1860s, South of Market,
with its upscale neighborhoods of Rincon Hill and South Park, was the fashionable
part of the city. William Ralston and Asbury Harpening were inspired to extend Montgomery Street south from
Market Street to China Basin and the bay. The pair visualized a
boulevard lined with trees and parks. Ralston and Harpening bought
the land from Market to Howard Streets, but were unable
to persuade landowners south of Howard to sell, stopping
the street's progress. Both lost millions for their efforts.
Today, New Montgomery deviates from the grid pattern
of streets and extends only those two blocks. It never
attained the grandeur envisioned by Ralston and Harpening.

*New Mont-
gomery Street
was not laid
out by the city,
but by private
ownership.*

## NIKITA KHRUSHCHEV

Soviet premier Nikita Khrushchev made a visit to the United States in 1959 that included a stop in San Francisco on September 20 and 21. During his stay, Khrushchev met with mayor George Christopher. Noticing the signs around town for Christopher's re-election campaign, Khrushchev offered to campaign for him. Christopher smilingly declined, shuddering to think what the endorsement of the leader of the Soviet Union would do to his campaign. After Christopher won the election on November 3, he received a cable of congratulations from Khrushchev.

*Khrushchev offered to campaign for Mayor Christopher's re-election.*

## NOB HILL

Bounded roughly by Bush, Stockton, Broadway, and Polk, Nob Hill has been one of the most prestigious addresses in the United States for over 100 years. Mining and rail barons of the 19th century, such as Mark Hopkins, Charles Crocker, Collis Huntington, and Leland Stanford, built their palatial mansions on what became known as the "Hill of Palaces." Most of the mansions of the rich and famous were brought down with the 1906 earthquake and fire, with the notable exception of James Flood's brownstone at Mason and California, now the Pacific Union Club. The hill today is populated by luxury hotels and upscale apartments, condominiums, and hotels such as the Stanford Court at 905 California, built in 1911 on the site of the Stanford mansion. Leland and Jane Stanford donated the money to establish Stanford University on the site of their horse-breeding ranch and country house in Palo Alto in 1890, in memory of their only child Leland, Jr., who died at the age of 15.

*According to local lore, the name Nob Hill comes from a contraction of nabob, British slang for those who became rich in India.*

## NORTH BEACH

The Briones family, who built their home and ranch near the present-day intersection of Powell and Filbert Streets in North Beach, supplied fresh meat and produce to passing ships before the Gold Rush. The North Beach neighborhood was named after a now long-vanished beach that once extended from Telegraph Hill to Russian Hill. It was built up by landfill soon after the Gold Rush. The waterfront extended to present-day Francisco Street. North Beach, centered on Columbus Avenue north of Broadway, is a diverse neighborhood with a lively mix of cultures. During the 19th century, it was largely industrial. In 1876, it contained 10 breweries. A substantial influx of Italians during the 1880s gave North Beach a secondary name of "Little Italy." By 1931, five Italian language newspapers were published in North Beach. The Chinese began crossing Broadway and moving into North Beach in the 1960s, and Asians are now the dominant ethnic group in the neighborhood. Nevertheless, tricolored Italian flags are still displayed on lampposts, and bocce ball, the Italian version of lawn bowling, is still enjoyed at the North Beach playground at Lombard and Mason Streets.

*Before the Gold Rush, North Beach was the home of Juana Briones and her family.*

## OCEAN BEACH

Before the invention of full-body wetsuits, San Francisco surfers at Ocean Beach protected themselves from the icy waters of the North Pacific by wearing layers of wool sweaters from Goodwill. The water is cold with a potentially fatal undertow, and the air is chilly, windy, and frequently encased in fog, but the beach is popular with bikers, joggers, and surfers. The city reserved Ocean Beach as public land in 1868. At the time, the only way to the Pacific shore was by expensive carriage rides, which were out of reach of the ordinary citizen. The Park and Ocean Railroad, opened in December 1883, charged only 10 cents to go to Ocean Beach, making it accessible for the first time to those of modest means. The Great Highway along the beach, completed in 1929, was built on top of a seawall started by John McLaren, superintendent of Golden Gate Park, to protect the park from the encroaching sand. Fort Funston, in the city's southwest corner, is a popular lift-off point for hang gliders.

*No one mistakes Ocean Beach for the Caribbean.*

## OLD CHINESE TELEPHONE EXCHANGE

The resplendent, pagoda-roofed Old Chinese Telephone Exchange at 743 Washington Street was completed in 1909. A branch of the Pacific Telephone and Telegraph Company's Chinatown Exchange, it was probably the most unusual telephone exchange in the country. The operators were required to have prodigious memories. They needed to be proficient in English and five Chinese dialects and were also obliged to learn every phone number of every one of the company's 2,400 clients because the Chinese believed it was rude to refer to a person as a number. Since there is no Chinese alphabet, the telephone directory was arranged by streets. The exchange closed in 1949 when rotary phones became commonplace. It is now a branch of the Bank of Canton and has been carefully preserved.

*The prized job of telephone operator at the exchange was frequently passed from mother to daughter.*

## OLD MINT BUILDING

Until 1937, the vaults at the Old Mint Building stored one-third of the nation's gold reserve. The precious metal was then transferred to Fort Knox, Kentucky. The 1874 Old Mint Building at Fifth and Mission Streets, the entrance of which is an imposing 12 feet above the sidewalk, was fortified with three-foot-thick granite walls and steel shutters. The sturdy construction saved the mint from the 1906 earthquake and fire, as did the efforts of soldiers and employees, who fought the flames for seven hours with a one inch hose tapped into basement cisterns. After the fire, the mint honored certificates issued by the city's destroyed banks, which allowed the city's residents access to cash. A new San Francisco mint opened in 1937 on Duboce Street. In 1966, it suffered a discrepancy of $15,000, all of it in quarters, which were stolen by employees. The Old Mint Building housed federal offices from 1937 until 1973, when it was converted to a museum. Although it has survived two major earthquakes, the building is considered by many experts to be unsafe and was closed for seismic upgrading in 1995.

*The Old Mint once housed one-third of the nation's gold reserve.*

## OLD ST. MARY'S CHURCH

Because of a shortage of building materials in the 1850s, the brick- and ironwork for St. Mary's Church at 660 California Street were brought from New England and the granite foundations imported from China. It was dedicated at midnight Mass on Christmas Day in 1854 and served as a cathedral until the new St. Mary's was built on Van Ness Avenue in 1891. That cathedral burned to the ground in 1962, and was replaced by the Cathedral of St. Mary at Geary and Gough Streets in 1971. Old St. Mary's now functions as a parish church. When it was built, it was the tallest building in San Francisco. The 90-foot clock tower contains the solemn admonition: "Son, Observe the Time and Fly from Evil." The message was aimed at those who frequented the 19th-century brothels across the street. The church interior has been gutted twice by fire, in 1906 and 1969, and restored both times.

*Old St. Mary's Church was the first Roman Catholic cathedral in California.*

## OLYMPIC CLUB

The Olympic Club, formed in 1860, is the oldest amateur athletic organization in the United States. The present building at 524 Post Street was erected in 1912. The glass-roofed swimming pool pavilion between the club and the Portman Hotel was added in 1906, right after the earthquake. Originally, fresh seawater was piped into the pool directly from the ocean six miles away. "Gentleman Jim" Corbett, a bank clerk and the club's boxing instructor, became heavyweight champion of the world when he defeated John L. Sullivan in 1892. Corbett held the title until 1897. The five-story brick clubhouse of the private club is equipped with a gymnasium, a solarium, squash and handball courts, an indoor track, a billiard room, dining halls, a library, and a lounge.

*Sid Cavill introduced the Australian crawl to America as the club's swimming instructor.*

## ON LOCATION

San Franciscans know that when Dustin Hoffman is shown driving across the Bay Bridge to Berkeley in the film *The Graduate* he's actually driving the wrong direction—into San Francisco. The house in *Pacific Heights* (1990) is not located in Pacific Heights, but in Potrero Hill at 19th and Texas Streets. It was selected for its views of the city. When filming began, it had been freshly painted, so the production company added an adhesive to make it look cracked and aged. The house lived in by Robin Williams and Sally Field in *Mrs. Doubtfire* (1993) is at 2640 Steiner Street in Pacific Heights. The church in *Sister Act* (1992) is at Valley and Church Streets in Noe Valley. To make the middle-class neighborhood look like a slum, the street was littered with trash and abandoned cars. In *Vertigo* (1958), Kim Novak lived at the Empire (now York) Hotel at 940 Sutter Street near Union Square and the Brocklebank Apartments across from the Mark Hopkins Hotel on Nob Hill. Filmed on the streets of San Francisco, *Bullitt* (1968) contains one of the most spectacular car-chase scenes ever filmed. Steve McQueen's car loses six hubcaps, and the same Volkswagen pops up repeatedly.

*In the 1967 film The Graduate, Dustin Hoffman is shown driving across the Bay Bridge to Berkeley.*

## ONLY CITY
## WITH CABLE CARS

Almost 100 other cities around the world once had cable cars, but all dismantled them as obsolete. San Francisco's beloved cable cars began operation on August 2, 1873, and immediately made an impact on the development of the city by opening previously inaccessible hilltop areas to residential use. By 1906, some 600 cars traveled the 110-mile route. After the advent of buses and private automobiles, the lines were reduced to a 12-mile network used by 44 cars. In 1947, city officials threatened to replace the cars with buses. A public backlash led to the preservation of the cars, and the constitution of the city now forbids discontinuation of the service. The Cable Car Barn and Museum at Washington and Mason Streets is the winding house for the underground cables that control the cars. The entire system runs out of this building. The cables wind around 14-foot-wide spinning drums and move in and out of the powerhouse on subterranean loops around the city at a constant 9.5 miles per hour. The cables that operate the cars have to be replaced as often as every 75 days, a task carried out overnight.

*San Francisco is the first and last city to operate cable cars.*

## PACIFIC UNION CLUB

City mining baron James Flood, who employed a man whose sole job was to constantly polish the $30,000 fence surrounding Flood's property, built the mansion that houses the Pacific Union Club at California and Mason in 1886. He chose brownstone, the first use of the material west of the Mississippi, because he admired the brownstone homes of his native New York City. It proved to be a fortuitous decision. The home was the only Nob Hill mansion that was not made of wood and, thus, the only one to survive the 1906 earthquake and fire. The interior was gutted, however, and Flood moved to Pacific Heights. His Nob Hill mansion was rebuilt in 1912 as the home of the private, exclusive, male-only Pacific Union Club. The third floor and semicircular wings were added in the 1912 remodeling.

*The bronze fence surrounding the club was patterned after a piece of lace favored by the wife of James Flood.*

## PAINTED LADIES

Originally, Victorians were painted in drab white, gray, black, and brown. The bay-windowed, decorated, redwood-framed Victorian houses, built from the 1870s through the turn of the century, are the city's most treasured architectural feature. Victorian houses fell out of favor for many years, and thousands that survived the 1906 fire were demolished or underwent alteration with new facades of asbestos sheeting, stucco, plaster, or stone. Much of the original decorative metalwork was stripped off during World War I and World War II scrap drives. Beginning in the 1960s, many Victorians were restored and renovated and were sold at exorbitant prices. About 14,000 of the original 48,000 Victorians are still standing in San Francisco. The highest concentration of Victorians is in an area bounded by Divisadero Street, Golden Gate Avenue, Webster Street, and Fell Street.

*Multicolored paint schemes on San Francisco's "Painted Ladies" did not become the fashion until the late 1960s.*

## PALACE HOTEL

President Harding died at the Palace Hotel in 1923. He had been suffering from high blood pressure and an enlarged heart, although some historians claim he was poisoned by his wife. The original Palace Hotel was opened by William Ralston in 1875. With 800 rooms, it was the largest and most luxurious of San Francisco's early hotels. The vast inner courtyard, called the Grand Court, could accommodate horse-drawn carriages. It had a glass dome with a catwalk overlooking a fountain and tropical gardens. The dining room was 150 feet long. The hotel, thought to be fireproof, was destroyed by the great 1906 conflagration despite a 28,000-gallon reservoir fed by four artesian wells. Famed opera star Enrico Caruso was staying at the hotel at the time and vowed never to return to San Francisco again. He kept his promise. The present Palace Hotel, now owned by the Sheraton chain, dates from 1909. The Garden Court contains 80,000 panes of intricately leaded art glass. The famous 1909 Maxfield Parish painting, *Pied Piper,* is framed in Maxfield's, an elegant bar on the premises.

*President Warren Harding died in room 8064 of the Palace Hotel on August 2, 1923.*

## PALACE OF FINE ARTS

The only building remaining from the 1915 Panama-Pacific International Exhibition, the Palace of Fine Arts is located at Baker and Beach Streets alongside a lagoon. San Francisco celebrated the opening of the Panama Canal and the city's revival from the 1906 earthquake by staging the fair in which 29 states and 24 nations participated. At the center was a tower covered with more than 100,000 cut-glass jewels imported from Bohemia. The fair drew more than 18 million visitors in 10 months. The exposition featured the tallest flagpole ever erected: a 299-foot, 52-ton, trimmed Douglas fir. Like other temporary fair buildings, the Palace of Fine Arts was originally constructed of inexpensive wood and plaster. It was so popular, however, that San Franciscans couldn't bear to dismantle it. Designed to look like a Roman ruin, the building deteriorated into a genuine ruin. Restored in 1962 with reinforced concrete, it serves as a 1,000-seat theater and also houses the Exploratorium, a hands-on science museum. A 1976 presidential debate between Jimmy Carter and Gerald Ford was held at the theater.

*During World War II, the Palace of Fine Arts was used as a warehouse for Army medical supplies.*

## PORTSMOUTH SQUARE

Author Robert Louis Stevenson's recollections of Portsmouth Square are included in his book *The Wreckers*. The square, on Grant Avenue between Washington and Clay Streets, was San Francisco's original plaza, laid out in 1839 under Mexican rule. It was initially only a block from the city's waterfront before landfill pushed the shore farther east. By 1844, the first official building, a customs house, was erected on the southwest corner of the square. It was here, following the United States declaration of war against Mexico, that the USS *Portsmouth* sailed into the bay in 1846 and Captain John B. Montgomery hoisted the American flag. The Mexican forces at the Presidio surrendered peacefully. The first American school was also erected on the square along with the city's first significant hotels. John Jenkins, accused of stealing a safe from a merchant, was lynched in the square in June 1851. He was the first victim of the Committee of Vigilance, established to halt the lawlessness of the Gold Rush era. Eventually, the city center shifted to the southeast, and Portsmouth Square declined in importance.

*Robert Louis Stevenson spent many hours writing in Portsmouth Square in 1879 and 1880.*

## PRESIDIO

Located at the entrance to the Golden Gate, the Presidio (Spanish for "garrison" or "fortress") has been a military installation for more than 200 years. In 1776, the Presidio was founded as a frontier station for the Spanish empire. In 1822, it became the northernmost outpost of the new Mexican republic, although the fort was in a perpetual state of disrepair. The United States took over after annexing California in 1846. During the Civil War, the Presidio was well fortified to protect California from invasion of Confederate forces. In the 1880s, the Presidio was planted with pine and eucalyptus trees, which eventually changed the sandy, treeless piece of coastline into a densely wooded area that now holds some 400,000 trees. The residents along Pacific Avenue had an agreement with the army stating that the tops of the cypress trees be kept trimmed so they would not block the view of the bay. The Presidio was decommissioned and transferred to the National Park Service's Golden Gate National Recreation Area in 1994. On the northern shore of the Presidio is Crissy Field, which served as a military aircraft testing site from 1919 to 1936.

*Lobos Creek, running from the Presidio's Mountain Lake to Baker Beach and the Pacific Ocean, is the only free-flowing stream remaining in San Francisco.*

## PSYCHEDELIA

Some of rock music's biggest and most psychedelic stars performed at the Fillmore Auditorium at Fillmore and Geary after Bill Graham, the most successful promoter of rock music in the United States, took over the 1912 yellow brick theater in 1965. Previously, it had been a dancing academy and church hall. The 1,000-capacity Fillmore was the venue for concerts by the Grateful Dead, the Jefferson Airplane, Janis Joplin, Jimi Hendrix, Led Zeppelin, and the Who. Cream recorded their live album *Wheels of Fire* at the auditorium. Six concerts a week were staged at the Fillmore during the 1967 "Summer of Love." Graham also opened the Avalon Ballroom at 1268 Sutter Street, now the Regency II Theater, and the Winterland at Post and Steiner Streets, torn down in 1985. Born Wolfgang Grojonca in Berlin, Graham escaped to the United States at the age of 10 during the Holocaust, which claimed his mother and two sisters. He died in a helicopter crash in 1991. The Bill Graham Auditorium in the Civic Center was named in his honor in 1992.

*The Fillmore Auditorium is perhaps best known for its legendary psychedelic light shows and the posters that promoted upcoming events.*

## RINCON CENTER

The old Rincon Annex Post Office
Building, completed in 1940, occupies
an entire city block bounded by Mission,
Spear, Howard, and Steuart Streets. When the post
office was moved, the building was transformed into a complex of offices, shops, and apartment towers, which opened in
1989. The center preserves the 27 historic murals, financed by the
WPA and painted by Russian-born artist Anton Refregier.
Ninety-one changes were made to gain federal approval of
the murals, including making a stout monk thinner. The
murals show the unflattering side of the city's history, such
as the Spanish conquering the Native Americans and the
violent labor disputes of the 1930s. The left-leaning slant
of the artwork upset the city's conservative citizens, who unsuccess-
fully demanded the removal of the murals.

*Rincon Center
is one of the
city's Art Deco
masterpieces.*

## RINCON HILL

The city's first millionaires built Greek Revival and Gothic homes on Rincon Hill between Second, Folsom, Spear, and Brannan Streets. The area's glory days were short-lived, however. In 1869, a deep slice was made through the 100-foot-high hill to ease traffic on Second Street between the Financial District and the waterfront. The cut in the hill sent the neighborhood into sudden decline, and by the 1880s and 1890s, the wealthy moved to Nob Hill and the huge residences they left behind were converted into rooming houses. Nothing is left of Rincon Hill's original mansions, as the 1906 earthquake and fire destroyed them. During the 1930s, the hill was almost leveled to anchor the west approach to the San Francisco–Oakland Bay Bridge.

*In the 1850s, Rincon Hill contained the most exclusive residential real estate in San Francisco.*

## RUSS BUILDING

The tan, terra-cotta-clad Gothic Russ Building is located at 225 Montgomery Street between Pine and Bush. When it opened in September 1927, its 31-story, 435-foot height made it the tallest building not only in San Francisco, but on the West Coast. Today, the Russ Building is dwarfed by the forest of downtown high-rises. Over 20 buildings in San Francisco are taller than this venerable structure. It was built atop a garage with space for over 400 cars, the first garage ever in an office building. The Russ family owned the property from 1847 until 1950. John Christian Russ, a German watchmaker, purchased the site, then a sandy spit of land on the shore, at an auction for $26. The family first built a home on the site, then two hotels and an office block before the erection of the Russ Building. The Russ family sold their $26 piece of property in 1950 for $2,739,000.

*From 1927 until 1964, the Russ Building was the tallest in San Francisco.*

## RUSSIAN HILL

The heart of Russian Hill is bordered by Broadway, Chestnut, Larkin, and Taylor Streets. It was first settled in 1852 by working-class families who built small wooden houses on the steep slopes. Late in the 19th century, a community of artists moved in, making Russian Hill San Francisco's first bohemian neighborhood. It did not become a popular place to live until the arrival of the cable cars between 1880 and 1891. About 400 acres of Russian Hill were saved from the 1906 fire because the area was sparsely populated and dotted with wells. In 1974, a 40-foot height limit was placed on buildings on Russian Hill to stop the invasion of high-rise apartment buildings. Movie producers love the neighborhood's precipitous hills and have used them for spectacular car chases. Many streets are too steep to pave and end in stairways. Macondray Lane is a pedestrian street off Jones between Green and Union. It was the model for Armistead Maupin's Barbary Lane in his serialized 1970s epic *Tales of the City*.

*According to legend, a crew of Russian fur traders, down from Alaska to hunt sea otters, buried their dead on the hill in the 1820s.*

## ST. MARY'S CATHEDRAL

The ultramodern St. Mary's Cathedral, built in 1971 and located at 1111 Gough at Geary Boulevard, is the third cathedral in the city to bear the name. The original, erected in 1854, is now known as Old St. Mary's Church in Chinatown. The second, on Van Ness Avenue at O'Farrell Street, was completed in 1891 and burned to the ground in 1962. The Catholic church wanted a hilltop site to replace the destroyed cathedral and coveted the Geary and Gough corner. A supermarket, built only a year earlier, was torn down and relocated to church property at Eddy and Laguna Streets. The dramatic, innovative cathedral can seat 2,500 with standing room for 2,000 more around a central altar under a glittering baldachino by sculptor Richard Lippold that features 7,000 aluminum rods that move in the slightest breeze and symbolize ascending prayer. Four floor-to-ceiling windows provide views of the San Francisco skyline.

*Some compare the cathedral's 189-foot white cupola to a washing machine agitator, earning it the nickname "St. Maytag."*

## ST. PATRICK'S CHURCH

St. Patrick's Church at 756 Mission Street was built in 1872 as a parish church for Irish immigrants, the dominant ethnic group in 19th-century South of Market. They worked in the factories, warehouses, and docks in the area. St. Patrick's, nicknamed "The Most Irish Church in America," was founded in 1851. Between 1854 and 1872, the congregation worshiped at a chapel on the site of the present Palace Hotel. The interior of the current church is decorated in the Irish national colors of green, white, and gold, and ancient Celtic patterns are embroidered on vestments. The regular worshipers are now mostly Filipino, and Mass is conducted in Tagalog. The church stands as a 19th-century monument in an area that has largely been leveled by postwar urban renewal programs.

*Scars of the 1906 earthquake fire that gutted the interior of St. Patrick's Church are still visible on the exterior walls.*

## STS. PETER AND PAUL CHURCH

The twin 191-foot spires of the Sts. Peter and Paul Church at 666 Filbert Street stand high above North Beach and Washington Square. Construction of the largest Catholic church in San Francisco began in 1922 and took 15 years to complete. In 1927, the church was the target of a bomb attack by a group of anarchists. The police foiled the attempt by killing the terrorists, who were given their last rites on the steps of the church they tried to destroy. On the first Sunday in October, the annual Blessing of the Fleet is celebrated with a Mass followed by a parade to Fisherman's Wharf. Joe DiMaggio married his first wife here, but wasn't permitted to marry Marilyn Monroe in the church in 1954 because both were divorced. Instead, they exchanged vows at City Hall and had their wedding photos taken at the church. Reflecting the ethnic diversity of North Beach, Mass is conducted in English, Italian, and Cantonese. When founded in 1884, the church was at Grant Avenue and Filbert Streets.

*Cecil B. DeMille filmed the construction of the church's foundation, using it for the building of the Temple of Jerusalem in his silent classic The Ten Commandments.*

## SANDLOT BASEBALL

In addition to *sandlot baseball,* other terms coined in San Francisco include *shanghai, Mickey Finn, hoodlum, psychedelic, hippie, beatnik, yuppie, blue jeans, denim, fortune cookie, cable car,* and *steam beer.* The term *sandlot baseball* dates from the 1860s when a cemetery that stood where the Civic Center is now located was converted into a park. A sand hill was leveled to create a 17-acre park, which became the training ground for San Francisco's young baseball players. The area became known as the "sandlots." San Francisco sportswriters dubbed the young athletes *sandlotters,* a term that spread across the country and was applied to amateur baseball players everywhere. San Francisco's first native-born major leaguer was Sandy Nava in 1882. San Francisco sandlotters who have reached baseball's hall of fame include Joe DiMaggio, Harry Heilmann, Joe Cronin, Tony Lazzeri, Frank Chance, and George Kelly.

*The term* sandlot baseball *originated in San Francisco.*

## SAN FRANCISCO ART INSTITUTE

The San Francisco Art Institute at Chestnut and Jones Streets in Russian Hill has played a key role in the development of contemporary art in San Francisco. Its distinguished faculty through the years has included the painters Clyfford Still and Richard Diebenkorn, and important visiting instructors such as Man Ray, Ad Reinhardt, and Mark Rothko. The school occupied the mansion built by Mark Hopkins and his wife Mary on Nob Hill from 1878 until it burned in 1906. It was donated to the school by Mary's second husband Edward Searles, an interior decorator 22 years younger than his wife. The two scandalized San Francisco society by marrying after Mark Hopkins's death. A gallery in the present complex on Chestnut Street contains a two-story mural painted in 1931 by famed Mexican artist Diego Rivera, titled *The Making of a Fresco Showing the Building of a City*. The building dates from 1926 with a 1969 addition. Some claim that the institute is haunted by a ghost living in the tower.

*Founded in 1871, the San Francisco Art Institute is the oldest art school west of the Mississippi.*

## SAN FRANCISCO MARRIOTT

The San Francisco Marriott at 777 Market Street opposite Grant Avenue near Moscone Center created an uproar when it opened. The 40-story zigguratlike construction topped with reflecting glass pinwheels that glow at sunset earned it comparison to a jukebox, a rectal thermometer, a pinball machine, and a parking meter. It looks as though it belongs in Las Vegas or on the set of The Wizard of Oz and has replaced the Transamerica Pyramid as the building San Franciscans love to hate. The ballroom of the hotel extends under Yerba Buena Gardens, which is bounded by Mission, Third, Howard, and Fourth Streets. The gardens are part of an urban renewal project that is the result of more than three decades of wrangling between politicians, developers, and private citizens. The centerpiece of the project is the memorial to Dr. Martin Luther King, Jr. It features illuminated glass panels with quotes from the civil rights leader in several languages and a huge waterfall 50 feet high and 20 feet wide.

*The San Francisco Marriott opened unexpectedly early in October 1989, serving as a shelter after the Loma Prieta earthquake.*

## SAN FRANCISCO MUSEUM OF MODERN ART

The San Francisco Museum of Modern Art did not have a building of its own until 1995. For the previous 60 years, the museum was located on the third and fourth floors of the Veterans Building in the Civic Center. Until 1976, it was known simply as the San Francisco Museum of Art. The San Francisco Museum of Modern Art at 151 Third Street between Howard and Mission Streets is one of the ten most-visited museums in the United States. The new facility houses over 17,000 works of art. Five floors of galleries are designed around a 125-foot cylindrical skylight finished with alternating bands of black-and-white marble and crossed by a footbridge on the top floor. It is considered one of the best examples of contemporary architecture in the city. The building was designed by Swiss architect Mario Botta, who intended to plant trees around the oculus at the top. Since the trees would be next to impossible to maintain and could be uprooted during high winds, the plan was abandoned.

*The San Francisco Museum of Modern Art was the first on the West Coast devoted to 20th century art.*

## SAN FRANCISCO–OAKLAND BAY BRIDGE

The original toll on the San Francisco–Oakland Bay Bridge was 65 cents per passenger, but if the car contained more than four passengers, each additional one was charged only five cents. The bridge was finished in 1936, six months before the completion of the Golden Gate Bridge. The west crossing is a double suspension bridge, while the Oakland side is a cantilever and truss design. A tunnel through Yerba Buena Island connects the two spans. Originally, the top deck was for two-way automobile traffic, and the bottom deck for trucks and commuter trains. The tracks were removed in 1958, and buses replaced the trains. In 1963, the current configuration began operation, with the top deck used for all westbound vehicular traffic and the bottom deck for traffic heading east. The lights strung across the steel cables of the bridge were installed for the 50th anniversary celebration in 1987 and intended to be temporary. They proved to be so popular that an extra 25 cents was added to the toll to make them permanent. During the 1989 earthquake, one section of the upper deck collapsed into the lower one, killing one person.

*When the San Francisco–Oakland Bay Bridge opened, there was little incentive to carpool.*

## SEA LIONS

Scientists are at a loss to explain why San Francisco's sea lions migrated en masse to Pier 39 from Seal Rocks following the 1989 earthquake. The sea lions also stayed away from Seal Rocks for two years after the Cliff House burned to the ground in 1907. California sea lions are found along the Pacific Coast between Santa Barbara, California, and Oregon. Beginning in 1990, they became one of Pier 39's prime tourist attractions when they moved to the pier from their rocky outpost. Drawing about 10 million visitors a year, Pier 39 is the third most popular destination in the country behind Disney World and Disneyland. At first, merchants at the shopping complex were aghast and wanted the animals removed, fearing a loss of business. They smelled, barked loudly, and polluted the water with their waste. Tourists loved them, however, and merchants soon discovered that the sea lions were actually good for business. The sea lion population varies from around 600 in January and February to virtually none in June and July when they head south to breed.

*Shortly after the 1989 earthquake, most of San Francisco's sea lion population moved from Seal Rocks just beyond the Cliff House to take up residence at Pier 39 on the bay.*

## SEALS STADIUM

California's first regular-season major league baseball game, a matchup between the San Francisco Giants and the Los Angeles Dodgers on April 15, 1958, was played at Seals Stadium before a capacity crowd of 23,192. Pitcher Ruben Gomez highlighted the Giants' 8–0 win with a complete game shutout. Prior to the 1958 season, the Giants played at the Polo Grounds in New York City. Seals Stadium, located at 16th and Bryant Streets, was the home of the minor league San Francisco Seals of the Pacific Coast League from 1931 through 1957. The Giants played at the stadium for two seasons until Candlestick Park opened in 1960. Seals Stadium was torn down shortly after the move.

*Seals Stadium held the state's first regular-season major league baseball game.*

## SHIP THAT INSPIRED JULES VERNE

The ship located at Pier 42 and once chartered by Jules Verne inspired the writing of Verne's book *Twenty Thousand Leagues Under the Sea*. Built in Bordeaux, France, in 1862, the Sailing Ship Restaurant was known as the *Ellen* during her days on the high seas. Before her reincarnation as a restaurant in the 1970s, the ship voyaged all over the world. During World War I, she was used for troop and supply transport and spy missions. During Prohibition, the *Ellen* had a stint running liquor from Canada to the United States. The ship was purchased by Columbia Pictures during the 1930s and used in such films as *Moby Dick* (1930), *Treasure Island* (1934), *Mutiny on the Bounty* (1935), *Captain Blood* (1935), and *Stowaway* (1936). Among those who starred on her decks were Clark Gable, Lionel Barrymore, John Barrymore, Shirley Temple, Basil Rathbone, and Errol Flynn.

*At the beginning of the century, the ship located at Pier 42 was chartered by Jules Verne.*

## SOURDOUGH BREAD

Isadore Boudin came to San Francisco in 1849 and four years later he opened the bakery where he produced his famous sourdough bread. Sourdough was invented by the Egyptians more than 4,000 years ago, but the white, crusty, slightly bitter, no-yeast loaf has become synonymous with San Francisco. There is no doubt that sourdough bread made in the city has a different taste than sourdough bread made anywhere else. Many aficionados assert that the unique, tangy flavor of the local bread can be attributed to the spores, fungi, and bacteria in the San Francisco air. Others claim the special taste of the bread is the result of the fog. Sourdough was a staple food in the Gold Rush days. Miners took sour starters with them on their travels to the extent that those who participated in the Alaska gold rush of the 1890s were called "sourdoughs." The Boudin Sourdough Bakery is still producing loaves of the popular bread.

*French immigrant Isadore Boudin was the first San Franciscan to produce sourdough bread.*

## SOUTH PARK

Oval-shaped South Park, between Second, Third, Bryant, and Brannan Streets, was built in 1854 in imitation of London's Berkeley Square. The park was once surrounded by mansions, filled with flowers, and enclosed by locked iron fencing to which only residents had a key. It was developed as a socially elite neighborhood by English financier George Gordon, but he never realized his dreams. Gordon suffered financial reverses and died penniless. Less than two decades later, the rich departed for Nob Hill. South Park gave way to rooming houses, factories, and warehouses and bottomed out as a skid row when the Bay Bridge was built. After more than a century of neglect, South Park is enjoying a revival as a restaurant, cafe, and shopping quarter. Many of its abandoned warehouses have been converted into artist lofts, apartment buildings, and offices for designers and computer startups.

*Georgian mansions originally surrounded South Park.*

## SPRECKELS MANSION

Spreckels Mansion occupies a full block, bounded by Washington, Jackson, Gough, and Octavia Streets. It originally had 26 bathrooms. The mansion was completed in 1913 for sugar magnate Adolph Spreckels. In 1908 at the age of 50, he secretly married 27-year-old Alma de Bretteville in Philadelphia. The six-foot-tall Alma was the model for the *Victory* statue atop the Dewey Monument in Union Square and became an enthusiastic patron of the arts. The building in the back of the mansion houses a covered pool, the largest private indoor swimming pool in the country. Alma took daily swims in the nude in the pool well into her 80s. White limestone has proved to be a poor choice for the construction of the home, because the city's moist climate has weathered it badly, seriously eroding the exterior. It doubled as a nightclub in the 1957 film *Pal Joey*. Romance writer Danielle Steel bought the mansion in 1990.

*The 55-room Spreckels Mansion is the largest private home in San Francisco.*

## SS JEREMIAH O'BRIEN

The SS *Jeremiah O'Brien* was named after the first American naval hero of the Revolutionary War. During World War II, liberty ships transported troops, food, tanks, gasoline, and ammunition to Allied battlefields. There were 2,751 built. The *Jeremiah O'Brien* was constructed in 57 days and launched in 1943 at Portland, Maine. Two hundred liberty ships were sunk during World War II, 500 were sold to European companies after the war, and the rest were scrapped after the Vietnam War. The *Jeremiah O'Brien* made 11 voyages during the Normandy invasion in 1944, and she returned 50 years later for the anniversary celebrations. Still in working order, the ship takes passengers on bay cruises twice each year. The third weekend of every month is "steaming weekend," when the engine is started while the ship remains at the dock.

*Located at Pier 32 on Brannan Street, the SS Jeremiah O'Brien is the last surviving unaltered World War II liberty ship.*

## STEEPEST STREETS IN
## SAN FRANCISCO

Filbert Street between Leavenworth and Hyde in the Russian Hill neighborhood and 22nd Street between Church and Vicksburg in the Noe Valley area are the two steepest streets in San Francisco. Both have a grade of 31.5 percent, which means that for every 100 feet of forward progress the street rises 31.5 feet. Although these and other hilly streets give San Francisco its appealing character, there is a downside. Drivers and passengers get cold feet when facing the initial descent, which gives the illusion of flying over the edge. Walking is no easy task. Ascending the steepest blocks of San Francisco is the equivalent of climbing a six-story building, although no one complains about the view at the top. Other steep streets include Jones between Union and Filbert (29 percent grade), Duboce between Buena Vista and Alpine (27.9 percent), Jones between Green and Union (26 percent), Webster between Vallejo and Broadway (26 percent), Duboce between Alpine and Divisadero (25 percent), Jones between Pine and California (24.8 percent), and Fillmore between Vallejo and Broadway (24 percent).

*Filbert Street and 22nd Street are the steepest in the city.*

## SUTRO BATHS

The largest of the Sutro Baths' seven public swimming pools was 300 feet long and 175 feet wide. Their creator, Prussian-born Adolph Sutro, arrived in San Francisco in 1851 at the age of 21 to seek Gold Rush riches, but made his fortune from silver and the Comstock lode in Nevada. Mining silver proved to be treacherous, so Sutro designed a four-mile-long tunnel beneath the silver vein that allowed miners better access to the lucrative seams. Returning to San Francisco, he sank his money into real estate and eventually owned one-twelfth of the land in the city. When Sutro opened his opulent Sutro Baths in 1896, there was room for 25,000 swimmers and spectators amid sculptures and ancient artifacts under a soaring glass dome. The baths had an assortment of slides, trapezes, and swings, 500 private dressing rooms, and restaurants on three levels. Visitors could see the ocean through a tunnel cut in the rocks or from behind 100,000 square feet of glass. Sutro Baths prospered for only about a decade, then gradually deteriorated. A suspicious fire destroyed the baths in 1966. The ruins can still be seen north of the Cliff House at the end of Point Lobos Avenue on land owned by the National Park Service.

*The Sutro Baths contained seven swimming pools that ranged in temperature from 50° to 110° F.*

## SUTRO HEIGHTS PARK

The bluff top overlooking the Cliff House and the Pacific Ocean was the site of the home of Adolph Sutro. A pair of stone lions and a statue of Venus are the main remnants of the mansion that was occupied by his daughter Emma until 1938 and demolished a year later. The land was bequeathed to the city as a public park. Sutro lavished most of his attention on the grounds of his estate, importing trees and flowers from all over the world. He designed a wind-powered watering system, constructed a large glass conservatory for delicate plants, and installed over 200 statues. Sutro opened his estate between nine and five o'clock each day so the public could stroll through the 20-acre grounds at their leisure. Since 1976, the park has been maintained by the Golden Gate National Recreation Area.

*The rock cliffs of Sutro Heights Park were reinforced with concrete and finished to look like real rock to prevent slides.*

## SUTRO TOWER

Before the Sutro Tower was completed in 1973, Bay Area residents were plagued by some of the worst TV reception in the nation because of the hilly terrain. The tower brought a surge of opposition because its prominent location atop Mt. Sutro marred the city's aesthetics. The red-and-white-striped tripod, which appears to have been constructed from an erector set, is visible for miles. On completion, the tower dramatically improved TV reception for most in the Bay Area, but actually ruined reception for those living nearby. Wind blowing through the tower emits an eerie noise which can awaken residents living close to Mt. Sutro. The tower is also the transmission point for many of San Francisco's FM stations and houses equipment for monitoring air pollution and meteorological conditions.

*At 981 feet, Sutro Tower is the tallest structure in San Francisco.*

## SWEDENBORGIAN CHURCH

The main architect of the Swedenborgian Church and its unusual bark-covered tree trunk supports was A. Page Brown. Others who collaborated in the conception of the church included Bernard Maybeck and Joseph Worcester, reverend of Swedenborgian Church, who was himself an architect and who personally selected the madrone for the ceiling. The wood-and-brick chapel at Lyon and Washington Streets in Pacific Heights is officially named the Church of New Jerusalem. The congregation's doctrinal inspiration was early 19th-century Swedish scientist, philosopher, and religious writer Emanuel Swedenborg. His values stressed personal development and tolerance and encouraged involvement in social issues. Completed in 1895, the church is designed along the lines of a simple log cabin, complete with a massive fireplace and rough-hewn wood beams. The church's doorway is reached by passing through a walled garden. Inside, the church has chairs, instead of pews, which were built by hand, without nails, of maple and woven tule rushes from the Sacramento River delta. The church is a popular setting for weddings of couples of all faiths and denominations.

*The ceiling of the Swedenborgian Church is supported by bark-covered trunks of California madrone from the Santa Cruz Mountains.*

## TELEGRAPH HILL

A telegraph station on Telegraph Hill once connected to a station at Point Lobos on the Pacific Ocean and alerted San Franciscans of ships approaching the port. Telegraph Hill, in the northeast corner of the city, looked quite different in the Gold Rush days. The east slope used to be smooth and round. The barren, jagged cliff visible today was formed in part by sailors digging out ballast for their empty ship holds during the Gold Rush era when the shore was located at the base of the hill. The rest of the hill was dug out for landfill and the construction of seawalls. The blasting of Telegraph Hill continued until 1911. Many homes were shaken from their foundations and crashed to the bottom 200 feet below. Until the 1930s, Telegraph Hill was still somewhat rural in appearance, and many streets, including Montgomery, were paved with dirt. Many of the pre-1906 houses survive because Italian residents refused to evacuate during the great fire and stayed to beat back the flames.

*Telegraph Hill drew its name from an electric telegraph station installed at its peak in 1850.*

## TEMPLE EMANU-EL

Temple Emanu-El is located at Lake Street and Arguello Boulevard in Presidio Heights. Rising 150 feet from the ground and visible for miles, Temple Emanu-El's orange-tiled, onion-shaped, Byzantine-style dome crowns a complex of offices and meeting halls. The building also incorporates mission revival architecture into the overall scheme. It was dedicated in 1926 as the third synagogue for the Emanu-El congregation, founded in San Francisco by Bavarian-born, German-speaking Jewish immigrants in 1850. The congregation's first two synagogues were located downtown. The second, at Sutter and Powell Streets, burned in 1906. The present temple seats more than 1,700 people and is lit by two stained-glass windows representing fire and water. Four massive bronze chandeliers symbolize the tears of the Jews.

*The dome of Temple Emanu-El was inspired by Constantinople's Hagia Sofia, a sixth-century Byzantine Church.*

## TERRIFIC PACIFIC

The stretch of Pacific Avenue between Columbus Avenue and Sansome Street earned the nickname "Terrific Pacific" due to rampant vice in the area during the Barbary Coast era. Every building along this street was once a saloon, gambling house, dance hall, or brothel. The vice that flourished in the Jackson Square area was shut down in 1917 by the same reformist movement that resulted in the enactment of Prohibition three years later. A smaller, tamer version of the Barbary Coast, called the International Settlement, limped on until the 1950s, but was considered disreputable enough to be off-limits to World War II soldiers and sailors. At 555 Pacific in the recessed vestibule of the old Hippodrome bar and dance hall are bawdy plaster bas-reliefs of dancing girls that shocked the Victorian sensibilities of the day. The Little Fox theater at 535 Pacific illegally housed a 60-foot distillery tank during Prohibition.

*Pacific Avenue between Columbus Avenue and Sansome Street was known as "Terrific Pacific."*

## TESSIE WALL'S TOWNHOUSE

Tessie Wall's townhouse at 535 Powell Street between Sutter and Bush Streets dates from 1911 and is the only surviving structure built downtown as a single-family residence. Wall became a flamboyant madam after divorcing her alcoholic fireman husband. Her famous parlor was at Powell and O'Farrell Streets in the Upper Tenderloin. She married gambler and political boss Frank Daroux in 1909 and moved into the house on Powell, but refused to give up her illicit profession despite repeated pleas from her new husband. Daroux divorced her and Tessie pledged that if she couldn't have him, neither would any other woman, and plugged him three times with a .22 caliber revolver. Daroux lived and moved to New York. Tessie sold her business for a small fortune and retired.

*Tessie Wall is credited with the oft-quoted line: "I'd rather be a lamppost on Powell Street than own all of San Mateo County."*

### TIN HOW TEMPLE

Tin How Temple on the fourth floor at 125 Waverly Place is the oldest Chinese temple in the United States. The present building dates from 1911. The temple is dedicated to Tin How, a woman born in China in A.D. 960, who is worshiped as the Queen of the Heavens and Goddess of the Seven Seas. She staged many miraculous rescues of sailors during the 10th century. The wooden statue of Tin How was brought to San Francisco from China during the Gold Rush. Tin How Temple is lit by red electric bulbs and burning wicks floating in oil. It houses religious symbols saved from temples destroyed during the 1880s when the Chinese were driven out of many small towns throughout northern California.

*Pioneer Chinese mariners grateful for their safe passage founded Tin How Temple in 1852.*

## TRANSAMERICA PYRAMID

The wings at the top of the Transamerica Pyramid hold elevators, emergency stairs, and a smoke tower. The geometric buttresses at the base were designed to give the building added strength in case of an earthquake. The 853-foot-tall Transamerica Pyramid is the dominant feature of the San Francisco skyline, but not just because it's the tallest building and comes into view unexpectedly throughout the city. The building caused great controversy when the plans were revealed because of its pyramidal shape and its prominent location at the end of Columbus Avenue. After it opened in 1972, the headquarters of the Transamerica Corporation was vilified as an out-of-scale brutalization of San Francisco's uniquely delicate skyline. Originally planned to be 1,000 feet in height, the pyramid was downsized because of the protests. The aesthetic appeal of this exotic centerpiece of downtown is still being debated, but the symbol gradually has become more acceptable to architectural purists. Adjacent to the pyramid on the east is Redwood Park, which has 80 redwood trees brought in from the Santa Cruz Mountains.

*The top 212 feet of the Transamerica Pyramid holds the building's utilities and is illuminated from within.*

## TRANSBAY TERMINAL

As many as 37 trains an hour left the Transbay Terminal building in the 1940s. The building, at First, Mission, and Fremont Streets was completed in 1939 as the terminal for the electric interurban trains that carried passengers over the Bay Bridge to the East Bay. It was originally known as the Bridge Terminal Building. Streetcars ascended the wide ramp, now used by buses, at First and Mission to discharge passengers on loading platforms with three pairs of tracks. To diminish noise, timber ties were embedded in concrete, which in turn rested on a two-inch insulated cushion. A viaduct carried the trains high above the streets to the lower deck of the bridge. The train service came to an end in 1958. The Transbay Terminal is used today by various regional bus companies with service to destinations such as Oakland, Lake Tahoe, and Reno.

*In the 1940s, nearly 90,000 people passed through the Transbay Terminal daily.*

## TREASURE ISLAND

Named after the Robert Louis Stevenson novel, Treasure Island was created to serve as the site of the Golden Gate International Exposition of 1939–40. The fair was a celebration of the city's simultaneous completion of the San Francisco–Oakland Bay Bridge and the Golden Gate Bridge. It was attended by 17 million. There were 13 states and 37 nations participating in the fair, including Italy and Japan. Less than 14 months after the close of the festivities, the United States was at war with both nations. The event is commemorated in the Treasure Island Museum, located in the Administration Building, one of three buildings from the exposition to survive. The island was partially constructed with stone removed from the Bay Bridge tunnel on adjacent Yerba Buena Island. It was scheduled to become San Francisco's airport, but was much too small for air traffic and too close to the bridges. Only Pan American Airways *China Clipper* seaplanes to Asia and the Pacific flew from the island.

*When it was completed in 1937, 400-acre Treasure Island was the largest man-made island in the world.*

## TWIN PEAKS

Twin Peaks, rising in the geographic center of San Francisco, provides an incomparable 360-degree view of the entire Bay Area. It is one of the few places in San Francisco where it is possible to see both the bay and the ocean. The two peaks are the second and third highest elevations in the city. Twin Peaks South is 910 feet above sea level, while Twin Peaks North stands at 904 feet. The Spanish called the peaks *Los Pechos de la Choca* (The Breasts of the Indian Girl). San Francisco's fog generally stops at Twin Peaks, Mount Davidson, and Mount Sutro, leaving the east side of the city warm and sunny. The city averages about 1,000 hours of fog each year, in some years more than 2,000 hours. Rolling in off the ocean, it can obliterate the 746-foot towers of the Golden Gate Bridge. One side of a hill will be encased in dense, bone-chilling fog, while the other is drenched in sun. There have been 10 measurable snowfalls in San Francisco since 1849. Seven of those were in the 19th century, with four of them coming in the 1880s. San Francisco registers the lowest average summer temperatures of any city in the country outside Alaska.

*The last snowfall in San Francisco occurred in 1976, when five inches fell at the top of Twin Peaks.*

## UNION SQUARE

In its early days, Union Square's garage offered valet parking, and the attendants, like firefighters, used metal poles to slide between parking levels. The square, bounded by Powell, Geary, Stockton, and Post, has long been the heart of San Francisco. The land for Union Square, as well as that for Washington Square, was donated to the city in 1850 by John Geary, who was elected the first mayor of San Francisco, on May 1, 1850. The name of the square stems from violent pro-Union rallies held there just prior to the Civil War, when there was some doubt whether California would support the Union or Confederate side. The Union Square area was largely residential and flanked by homes and churches until the 1890s when the area became the city's retail center. The 97-foot Corinthian column in the center of the square was erected in 1903 to celebrate the 1898 victory of Admiral George Dewey's fleet during the Spanish-American War. The column was originally on a larger base and was 12 feet shorter.

*The four-level parking garage beneath Union Square, opened in 1942, was also designed as a bomb shelter.*

## VAILLANCOURT FOUNTAIN

Vaillancourt Fountain, designed by Canadian artist Armand Vaillancourt, was placed in the Justin Herman Plaza of the Embarcadero Center in 1971. The configuration of 100 large, angled, abstractly arranged concrete tubes and boxes contains walkways and stairs that allow people to walk through without getting soaked. The fountain is hated by many and appears as though it's been disheveled by an earthquake. One wag said it looks like a deposit left by a gigantic dog with square bowels. During a free unannounced concert by the band U2 in the plaza in 1987, lead singer Bono angered San Francisco officials by spray-painting the fountain at a time when the city was conducting an antigraffiti campaign. The scene is immortalized in the band's 1989 movie *Rattle and Hum*. In retaliation, Vaillancourt flew from Montreal to paint the front of the stage at a U2 concert at the Oakland Coliseum.

*Due to droughts, the water in the Vaillancourt Fountain is frequently turned off.*

## WASHINGTON SQUARE

Bounded by Filbert, Union, Columbus, and Stockton, Washington Square contains a statue of Benjamin Franklin, a gift to San Francisco in 1879 from H. D. Cogswell, a millionaire dentist who preached against the evils of alcohol. He vowed to build one public fountain for every saloon in San Francisco in the hopes that the water from the facilities would keep the minds of the citizenry off booze. A time capsule was placed underneath the statue when it was installed. The capsule was opened in 1979 and replaced by another, which will be unveiled in 2079. The 1879 capsule was filled with temperance literature. The capsule buried in 1979 is said to contain some Levi jeans, a bottle of wine, a recording of Hoodoo Rhythm Devils, and a poem by Lawrence Ferlinghetti. The square was designated a public park in 1847, but was filled with unkempt cemeteries during the 1850s. The park is now the social center of the North Beach community.

*Every 100 years, a time capsule is buried in the square.*

## WINDMILLS

The Dutch Windmill, in the northwest corner of Golden Gate Park within sight of the Pacific Ocean, was built in 1902 to supply part of the water needed to keep the greenery alive and well by tapping into an underground stream. It once pumped 20,000 gallons of water per hour to the reservoir on Strawberry Hill. The windmill was erected because the Spring Valley Water Company, which supplied the city with water, charged exorbitant rates. The Murphy Windmill, in the southwest corner of the park, was added in 1905. When the city bought the water company in 1930, the windmills were no longer necessary and eventually fell into disrepair. In 1981, the Dutch Windmill was restored, but no longer pumps water and is merely a decorative accoutrement to the park. The Murphy Windmill has not been restored.

*Golden Gate Park requires about 5 million gallons of water a day.*

## WORLD'S LARGEST
## HOTEL LOBBY

Built in 1973 at 5 Embarcadero Center, the Hyatt Regency Hotel and its lobby were featured in the films *The Towering Inferno* (1974), *High Anxiety* (1978), and *Time After Time* (1979). The hotel building by John Portman and Associates has received national recognition for outstanding and innovative design. The 17-story atrium is filled with plants and trees. Greenery spills from the balconies. A four-story sculpture, *Eclipse*, by Charles Perry soars from the reflecting pool. The restaurant and bar at the top of the hotel rotates 360 degrees every 40 minutes, giving guests a truly panoramic view of the bay and city skyline. The Embarcadero Center, developed by the Rockefeller family, was initially referred to as "Rockefeller West," but the name didn't sit well with many San Franciscans because of its New York connection.

*The Hyatt Regency contains the world's largest hotel lobby: 300 feet long, 170 feet wide, and 170 feet high.*

## YERBA BUENA ISLAND

In 1931, San Franciscans decided Goat Island was too undignified a name to anchor and connect the new Bay Bridge and convinced the U.S. Geographic Board to change it to Yerba Buena Island. It was not the first time there was confusion over the name of the island. Spanish naval lieutenant Juan Manuel de Ayala gave present-day Yerba Buena Island the name *La Isla de Los Alcatraces* (Island of the Pelicans) in 1775, but an English sea captain drew a map in 1826 mistakenly naming the island on which the prison now stands as Alcatraz. In the 1870s, the Central Pacific Railroad proposed constructing a rail bridge to Yerba Buena Island from Oakland. Docks were to be built on the island to allow goods to be transferred from train to ship en route to destinations around the world. The idea was abandoned in favor of building harbor facilities at the Oakland Estuary. Yerba Buena Island became the stepping-stone between the cantilever and suspension sections of the Bay Bridge in the 1930s. It is connected to man-made Treasure Island by a 900-foot causeway. The tunnel opening, at 540 feet tall and 58 feet in diameter, is the largest in the world.

*Yerba Buena Island was officially named Goat Island by the U.S. Geographic Board in 1895 and remained that way until 1931.*

**JOHN SNYDER**

John Snyder is a sportswriter and the author
of *Play Ball, Basketball!, Goal!,* and *Hockey!,* all published by Chronicle Books. He lives in Cincinnati but left
his heart in San Francisco.